DEVELOPING
A POWERFUL
PRAYING CHURCH

Dr. Richard Blackaby
Rev. Rick Fisher

Blackaby Ministries International

Jonesboro, Georgia

DEVELOPING A POWERFUL PRAYING CHURCH
PUBLISHED BY BLACKABY MINISTRIES INTERNATIONAL
P.O. Box 1035
Jonesboro, GA 30237
www.blackaby.org

ISBN 978-0-692-88597-0

Publisher's Cataloging-in-Publication data

Names: Blackaby, Richard, 1961-, author. | Fisher, Rick T., author.
Title: Developing a powerful praying church / Richard Blackaby and Rick Fisher
Description: Includes bibliographical references | Jonesboro, GA: Blackaby Ministries International, 2017.
Identifiers: ISBN 978-0-692-88597-0 | LCCN 2017911951
Subjects: LCSH Prayer--Christianity. | Spiritual life--Christianity. | Church growth. | BISAC RELIGION / Christian Church / General | RELIGION / Christian Life / Prayer | RELIGION / Christian Ministry / General | RELIGION / Prayerbooks / Christian
Classification: LCC BV4501.2 .B5375 2017 | DDC 248.3--dc23

Printed in the United States of America
2017 — 1st ed

Contents

PREFACE

Pastor, is your church all God intends for it to be? If not, what would you be willing to do to see God transform it? What price would you pay? What adjustments would you make? What pain would you endure? What cross would you take up? Just how fervently do you want God do a mighty work in your congregation?

Today, the Church is under siege. Secular forces in society make a mockery of God's word. They brazenly transgress His commands. They vigorously oppose Christian morals. This reality alone would be troubling, but the situation is much worse. For evil forces not only surround the Church, they have infiltrated it. God's people have become enamored with the world. They have embraced its goals and values. Many professed Christians today are uncertain if they believe God's word or accept His standards.

God assigns pastors to congregations filled with such people. He commands these pastors to exhort their flock to holy living. They are instructed to lead their people to be salt and light in an increasingly dark age. Theirs is no small undertaking. So we ask the question again: What would you be willing to do to help your church become all God intends for it to be?

What if the key to a successful pastorate was prayer?

You may quickly interject, "But I *do* pray!" True enough. But have your prayers been sufficient? Jesus said that if we asked, we *would* receive. If we sought, we *would* find. If we knocked, the door *would* be opened to us (Matt. 7:14). Do Jesus' statements reflect your experience? Was He telling the truth?

God's word is our guidebook for the Christian life and for pastoral leadership. It is absolutely true. So why are so many pastors praying but not receiving?

Could it be that many pastors are not praying in the manner Jesus prescribed? Saying prayers is not the same as biblical intercession. Many churches are uttering prayers, but too few are crying out to God. We believe God's answer for the Church is found in prayer. But not the type and quality of prayer churches commonly practice today.

The key is to pray like Jesus did. Such prayer does not come easily. It differs from what many of us grew up experiencing. It requires sacrifice. It demands our full attention and commitment. But it is worth it! God's greatest movements throughout history, without exception, have been characterized by such prayer. Our hope is that God will use this book to kindle a burning desire within your soul to become a person who prays with the same depth, fervency, and faith as Jesus did.

We have both been pastors. We love God's people, and we are passionate about moving them from where they are to where God wants them to be. We have spoken in numerous pastors' and prayer conferences around the world. In the following pages we will share truths that have profoundly shaped us and that have exerted a huge impact on churches around the world. Please read the following chapters carefully and prayerfully. We believe that as you do, you may encounter the answers you have been seeking as you strive to lead a God-honoring, world-impacting church. We pray you do.

CHAPTER ONE

The Minister: Leading Out of the Overflow

INTRODUCTION

Few preachers have exerted as much influence on evangelical pastors in the modern era as Charles Haddon Spurgeon. Though he died in 1892, his sermons and books are still printed in large numbers and his portrait, perhaps more than any other mortal, graces the walls of ministers' studies. This is unsurprising, for Spurgeon developed the first megachurch. Ministering in London for 37 years, Spurgeon grew the Metropolitan Tabernacle to 5,500 in attendance, adding more than 15,000 members during his illustrious ministry. People required a ticket to attend the weekly church services, for the massive auditorium was often inadequate to accommodate the throngs who wished to hear the famous preacher.

Spurgeon is most famous for his powerful preaching, although he developed numerous other ministries, including an orphanage and a pastor's college. Yet Spurgeon believed the secret to his phenomenal success was not his preaching, but prayer. For many years his church's Monday evening prayer service averaged 3,000 in attendance. He loved to pray. Spurgeon declared: "Of course the preacher is above all others distinguished as a man of prayer. He prays as an ordinary Christian, else he were a hypocrite. He prays more than ordinary Christians, else he were disqualified for the office."[1] Though his personal library boasted more than 30,000 volumes, he confessed, "All our libraries and studies are mere emptiness compared to our closets."[2]

Many pastors would love to lead a church as large and influential as Spurgeon's was. Preachers long to have their auditoriums as full and their sermons published and as widely read as Spurgeon's. Yet far fewer pastors take personal and corporate prayer as seriously as Spurgeon did. Today's pastors often bemoan the fact that the people in their congregations are disinterested in prayer. However, pastors routinely confess that they themselves spend inadequate time praying.

Charles Spurgeon recognized that prayer was not something pastors could delegate. If a minister expects

---

[1]Charles Spurgeon, Lectures to My Students, 40.
[2]Ibid., 41.

his people to pray, he must be a person of prayer first. For a pastor cannot lead people where he has not been himself. Spurgeon concluded: "The minister who does not earnestly pray over his work must surely be a vain and conceited man . . . The preacher who neglects to pray much must be very careless about his ministry. He cannot have comprehended his calling. He cannot have computed the value of a soul, or estimated the meaning of eternity."[3] Numerous studies reveal that the only common denominator of revivals throughout history has been prayer. It is not surprising therefore that Spurgeon's church experienced continuous revival over the course of his lengthy tenure. His was a praying church and, as a result, it experienced unprecedented revival and growth.

If ministers are to grow a powerful praying church, they must lead in two specific ways. The first is in their personal self-mastery. They must develop their own prayer life so it is powerful, vibrant, and profoundly attractive to others. The second is in their corporate leadership of their congregation. Pastors must accept responsibility for deepening their people's prayer life until the church is a Spirit-filled, dynamic, world-changing center of intercession. In the remainder of this chapter we will look at ways pastors, by their own personal prayer life, can deeply impact their church. In a later chapter, we will examine practical ways pastors can lead their congregation to become a Christ-honoring, darkness-dispelling, center of prayer.

---

[3]Ibid., 47.

I. THE PROBLEM

The church has a major problem. It doesn't pray as it should. Jesus promised His disciples that if they asked, they would receive (Matt. 7:7). But today, despite this enormous promise, church prayer meetings, if they exist at all, are generally the least attended gathering of the week. Christ promised that the Church would have an open door to Him and His resources (Rev. 3:8). Yet churches disband by the thousands each year because they do not have the resources to continue. God promised that if His people called to Him, He would show them great and mighty things that they did not know (Jer. 33:3). Yet many churches today are unable to meet the challenges presented by an increasingly complex world. When church members are asked why they don't pray, they confess they don't know how, or they are too busy, or they see it as ineffectual. Surely if they believed God answered prayer, they would make time to pray. Numerous studies have demonstrated that healthy, growing churches are characterized by, among other things, prayer. Yet many churches don't pray, even when they are desperate. Churches know the solution to their problems, but they are not embracing God's answer.

Furthermore, churches typically look to their pastor to solve their problems. Whatever the church lacks, the pastor is supposed to provide. As its leader, churches expect its pastor to be exemplary in every aspect of the Christian life. Whether it is prayer, evangelism, Scripture memorization, or fasting, the church expects the pastor be a role model. This is where the problem intensifies.

Many pastors are not exemplary intercessors. In survey after survey, pastors confess that they pray far less than they should. They offer several reasons. For one, their churches often place heavy demands on their schedule, leaving little time to pray. Churches are performance driven. They want pastors to deliver entertaining, high-tech sermons. They expect their minister to visit every church member in the hospital and to be available 24-7. The early apostles declared that their priorities were prayer and preaching God's word (Acts 6:4). Yet rarely do churches insist that their pastor carve out significant time each week for prayer.

Not prioritizing prayer leads to a second problem. Many pastors don't know how to pray. Sure, pastors can wax eloquent from the pulpit offering up public invocations. But leave a pastor alone in a prayer room for an hour and many would not know how to spend the time. There are two reasons for this problem. First, many pastors have never been taught how to pray. And, sadly, when given the opportunity to learn, they typically forgo it. Senior pastors flood to seminars on church growth, but tend to send appointees to prayer conferences. Second, our prayer life flows directly out of the vibrancy of our relationship with God. Many pastors neglect their walk with God as they diligently attempt to fulfill the numerous tasks their congregation demands of them. As a result, the flock is left with an under-praying pastor tasked with helping the congregation improve their prayer lives. This process is clearly doomed to failure.

Pastors must ask themselves, "If the people in my congregation follow the example of my prayer life, what kind of church will I have?" If pastors are to develop vibrant, powerful, praying churches, they must have a vibrant, powerful prayer life themselves. Pastors cannot delegate prayer leadership to the women's organization or to a devout widow. It is primarily the pastor's responsibility. So, this is the question: how can pastors improve their prayer life so it exerts a dynamic influence on their congregation?

II. DEEPENING A MINISTER'S PRAYER LIFE

The greatest thing ministers can do for their people is cultivate their own prayer life so it is rich, fresh, Spirit-filled, and growing. The more they receive from God, the more they must give to others. The following are six ways ministers can enrich their prayer life:

1. Make Abiding in Christ a Lifestyle (John 15:1-11)

The power of ministers' public ministry depends on how they commune with God privately. Jesus explained this process by saying, *"I am the vine; you are the branches. The one who remains in me and I in him produces much fruit, because you can do nothing without Me"* (Jn. 15:5). It is out of our intimate, growing walk with Christ that our life exerts influence on others.

Many hard-working ministers have labored for Christ without abiding in Him. Theirs is a ministry of good works. They know little about abiding. Yet the quantity and quality of the fruit we produce in our ministry is directly related to the depth of our relationship with Christ. Jesus Himself declared that apart from abiding in Him, we could do *nothing* (John 15:5). Numerous ministers today do not believe this truth. Such people disdain spending quiet time with their Lord. They cite their busy schedules and the demands of their office for the paucity of their prayer life. The truth is, they believe much fruit can indeed be gained by their efforts. They neglect time with God so they can gain more "results." But this is the reality: pastors might grow attendance, but only Christ can build the Church (Matt. 16:18). Pastors who truly want to participate in God's work will spend regular, prolonged, intimate time abiding in Christ.

A Pastor Who Heard from God

As the pastor of a congregation with more than 1,000 attendees each weekend, I (Rick) found myself increasingly focused on what I could do to reach more people and exert a greater influence on our community. With a large budget and a healthy conference expense account, I could easily chase the next great thing, hoping to find the magic bullet in a program or strategy. In the midst of this pursuit, I chose to attend a conference in San Diego, California, that promised "innovative solutions" to the challenges pastors and churches face. To be honest, I'm not sure whether I chose this specific conference based on the content or the location. San Diego seemed like a great place to chase after the dream!

On a beautiful southern California day, I reluctantly made my way to a breakout session focused on impacting your community. With visions of walking along the boardwalk and gazing out on the Pacific Ocean with my wife following the session, I sat in the back row near the door (It's always good to plan an escape route!). At the beginning of the session, the speaker read Matthew 9:35-38. As I heard those words, the Holy Spirit spoke directly to my heart. He simply but powerfully said, "Rick, you have not been looking at the people surrounding your church community as I have. You are not seeing what I am seeing. If you were, you would join Me in what I am already doing around you." Immediately, I understood. I was not seeing what Jesus saw because I had not asked Him to help me see my community as He did. My prayer life was stale and barren. I was merely going through the motions.

I don't remember anything more the speaker said that day. God had captured my attention. I simply and humbly prayed, "Lord, I need to hear from you.

I want to hear from You because I want to see like You." My pen came alive in my hand as I scribed everything the Father was saying, the words He had desired to speak so many times before when I was too distracted to listen. Those notes morphed into a sermon series on the Matthew passage. I invited our congregation to pray and seek God's perspective on our community. We asked Him to help us notice what He was seeing around us, to help us view people as "harassed and helpless, like sheep without a shepherd." We asked Him to show us how and where to join His activity. After a series of sermons and two months of corporate prayer, God revealed His agenda to us. We joined Him in several specific ways and watched as He changed our lives and our community. The beginning of the transformation occurred when I stopped chasing and started seeking and listening.

Pastor, can we be candid? We speak in many prayer conferences around the country. The senior pastors are often noticeably absent at such meetings. Their people may be there in force. They may have appointed their associates to represent them. But they clearly believe they have more important things to do than learn how to improve their prayer life. Yet the most important thing ministers can do for their ministry is cultivate a deep walk with God. We can only imagine what might happen if congregations witnessed their pastors sitting on the front row of every prayer conference, diligently taking notes and earnestly seeking how God might make them a better intercessor for their people.

The problem for many ministers is that their congregation does not evaluate their performance by how much time they spend communing with Christ, but by whether they preach entertaining sermons, draw growing crowds, and bring in large offerings. No one sees their pastor on his knees in prayer, but everyone hears him preach. Ministers are therefore tempted to invest their time in areas people notice rather than on matters they do privately. But the truth is, though your people may not see you pray, they will certainly experience the results of your prayer life.

The reason abiding is so crucial for ministers is because our service for Christ is based entirely upon our relationship with Christ. The moment our relationship with Christ suffers, our service deteriorates. Jesus clearly understood this truth. Scripture states, *"He also named them apostles—to be with Him, to send them out to preach, and to have authority to drive out demons"* (Mark 3:12). Jesus' first invitation is always to a relationship. Jesus drew His disciples to Himself before He sent them out to minister to others. If the disciples had not first spent time with Jesus, they would have had no power or message to give others.

A second reason ministers must abide in Christ is because they experience unquenchable joy from that relationship. Jesus told His disciples, *"I have spoken these things to you so My joy may be complete in you and your joy may be complete"* (John 15:11). Ministry can be difficult. Countless ministers have burned out and quit in discouragement. Yet in God's presence is abundant joy (Ps. 16:11). Invariably, ministers who bitterly resign from their calling are people who frequently neglected to draw near to their Lord. It is impossible to abide in Christ's presence and remain discouraged!

Dwelling in Christ's presence fills the minister's heart with His love, joy, and divine power. Every time ministers pray publicly the congregation can discern the depth of their relationship with Christ. Therefore, they must jealously guard and cultivate time with their Lord.

2. Schedule Regular, Uninterrupted, Unhurried Time in Prayer

Ministers with a barren devotional life will have nothing of consequence to say to God when they pray publicly. E.M. Bounds declared: "No man can do a great and enduring work for God who is not a man of prayer, and no man can be a man of prayer who does not give much time to praying."[4] Ministers who long to spend time with their Master must proactively schedule time to be with Him. Scripture exhorts us to pray without ceasing (1 Thess. 5:17). Private times invested in the

---

[4]E.M. Bounds, *Power Through Prayer* (Grand Rapids: Baker Book House, 1972; reprint ed. 1982), 52-53.

prayer closet cultivate the spirit of continuous prayer throughout the day.

Prayer is not identical to Bible study. Pastors would often rather study their Bible or prepare sermons than pray. Sadly, many ministers spend far more time monitoring their social media accounts than they do communing with their Lord. For a prayer time to be powerful, it must have several characteristics. *First*, it must be *scheduled*. A minister's prayer life cannot be haphazardly squeezed into the occasional open spot on the calendar. People schedule important activities. If you would put an appointment with a congregant on your calendar, then surely you should deem God worthy of a calendar entry as well. Prayerlessness is not a time issue but a priority issue.

Second, it is *daily*. Ministers who think they can serve their Master without communing with Him daily grossly overestimate their ability and underestimate the power of prayer. Abraham took matters into his own hands for one day and people continue to suffer the consequences thousands of years later. Moses took control for one day and it cost him forty years in a wilderness! (Ex. 2:11-15). People who do not prioritize time with their Lord fail to understand both the enormous good that results from walking in step with the Spirit and the painful consequences of living one day outside God's will. Congregants need assurance that when their pastor ministers to them, he has already spent rich time in God's hallowed presence.

Third, it must be *private*. Some ministers like to spend their devotional times in coffee shops or other public places. Certainly, prayer in such venues is excellent for interceding for those on the premises. But the kind of intimate, agonizing, soul-searching, glory-falling prayer we are talking about is best conducted without an audience. Extroverts tend to like being around people and their accompanying noises. But should you truly grasp the magnitude of the One you are meeting with in prayer, you will soon recognize that everyone else fades into the background (Rev. 1:9-17). Once you learn to commune with the risen Christ, every other human voice will be nothing more than an unwelcome intrusion.

Fourth, it must be *undistracted*. When you prepare to pray, close your door, shut down your computer, and mute your phone. When you talk with the Almighty, He deserves your full attention. The reason some people feel compelled to augment their time with God is because they do not grasp the awesome reality of who they are meeting. When you talk with the King, you do not need music playing softly in the background for your conversation to be meaningful! The more clearly you learn to hear God's voice, the less patient you will be with any competing sounds. It is best to meet with God in a location that is barren of distractions. Do not insult God by turning your attention away from Him every time you receive an electronic message! Remove every distraction so nothing interferes with the most important appointment of your day.

Fifth, it must be *adequate*. You insult your Creator when you distractedly hurry in and out of His presence! Your prayers will never have the proper impact on you or others if you continually check the time so you are not late for your next appointment. You should schedule enough time with your Lord each day so you are unhurried in His presence. Carving out adequate time will demand discipline and wise choices on your part. You may need to wake up early in the morning or stay up late into the night. If you struggle to rise early in the morning, forgo late night television or social media. Be prepared to adjust your schedule in whatever way necessary so you are fully alert and available to God when you meet with Him.

3. Seek God's Heart and Mind (1 Sam. 2:35).

Prayer is not primarily an avenue for you to express your concerns to God. Rather, it is God's divinely orchestrated means of laying His heart over yours. You do not know everything your congregation is facing, but God does. You do not understand what God intends to do in and through your church, but He does. What God has to say in prayer is infinitely more important than what you want to discuss. For that reason, you must approach prayer with a desire to learn what is on God's heart and mind.

God declared: *"Then I will raise up a faithful priest for Myself. He will do whatever is in My heart and mind"* (1 Sam. 2:35). We are not called to do what we think is best for the Lord. We are servants. Our calling is to do our Master's bidding. We cannot know God's will unless He shares it with us. As we pray, the Lord will place people, situations, and issues on our heart. Once we know what is on God's mind, we have our marching orders.

Prayer on Monday, Answer on Wednesday

One Monday morning I (Richard) was in my pastoral office praying for my congregation. I knew of many of the needs my people had, but I was unaware of other issues. As I prayed, the Holy Spirit brought my attention to a young couple. I knew the wife suffered from health issues and they did not have much money. As I prayed, I sensed the Lord asking me to do more than intercede. I felt led to pull out some stationary and write them a note. I told them God loved them and had a wonderful future in store for them. I assured them they could trust the Lord's leading in their lives. I mailed the letter to the couple later that day.

Two days later I was in the office when my phone rang. The man I had written was calling. His first words were, "How did you know?" Apparently he had gone to work that morning and unexpectedly been laid off, effective immediately. He had no money to pay his monthly expenses. He was in shock as he arrived home. He had no idea how he would tell his wife the devastating news.

As he approached his apartment, the man noticed the mailman putting letters into his mailbox. One of the letters was from his pastor. He realized his pastor had been praying for him and had felt God lead him to send a message. "How did you know?" the man asked me that Wednesday. "I didn't," I replied. "But on Monday morning I was talking with someone who did." Spending regular time in prayer gives God the opportunity to share what He knows is coming so you can join Him in His work.

---

4. Pray to See God More Clearly (Rev. 1:9-17).

No one on earth knew Jesus as well as the apostle John did. John had walked with Jesus for more than three years. John witnessed Jesus walk on water, feed 5,000 people, and raise the dead. John saw Jesus' transformation on the Mount of Transfiguration. He stood before the crucified Christ at Calvary. He was one of the first to witness the empty tomb and the risen Christ. John watched Jesus ascend into heaven. Few people in history had ever witnessed as much of Jesus as John had.

As a prisoner on the Isle of Patmos, he was the lone surviving apostle. As he was praying on the Lord's Day, John had an unprecedented encounter with Christ (Rev. 1:9-16). So awesome and terrifying was the sight of the risen Christ that the aged apostle fell to the ground as a dead man (Rev. 1:17). Can pastors who have served the Lord for decades encounter Christ in new ways as they pray? Yes. Though we may have studied the Bible for ten thousand hours and uttered ten thousand prayers, each time we bow our head in prayer we have the opportunity to be swept into a breathtaking encounter with the risen Christ that is unlike anything we have previously experienced. Do you need a fresh encounter with Christ today?

No one in heaven is discouraged. No pessimists are gathered before God's celestial throne. In heaven, people see God clearly. It is impossible to truly know God and to lose hope or become discouraged. A.W. Tozer declared, "The man who comes to a right belief about God is relieved of ten thousand temporal problems . . . So necessary to the Church is a lofty concept of God that when that concept in any measure declines, the Church with her worship and her moral standards declines along with it. The first step down for any church is taken when it surrenders its high opinion of God."[5]

Prayer helps the minister understand God's character and nature. As we pray, we encounter His holiness, power, and love. The better we know Him, the more effectively we can represent Him to others. If we do not understand how holy God is, we will not denounce sin as fervently as we ought. If we do not recognize how powerful God is, we may grow discouraged or assume what He asks is impossible. If we do not fathom God's love, we will worry that God might not adequately provide for us. If we do

---

[5]A.W. Tozer, *The Knowledge of the Holy* (New York: Harper One, 1961), 2, 4.

not comprehend God's grace, we will become impatient and unforgiving of others. To represent God well, we must know Him intimately.

When ministers begin to worry, fear, or become discouraged, they are clearly not spending adequate time in God's presence. If they were, they would better understand the awesome nature of the God they serve and represent. Over the years, we have ministered to many church leaders who were struggling. Not once have we met a discouraged pastor who was experiencing a vibrant prayer life. A fearful, worrisome, discouraged pastor is someone who is failing to pray as they ought.

5. Pray for Surrender (Matt. 26:39).

God is absolutely trustworthy. He loves us infinitely. His awesome power holds the universe together. He knows the future. Each of His purposes will come to pass exactly as He ordained them. Nevertheless, we struggle at times to trust and obey Him.

Christ has a resounding answer for each of your church's problems. No personal challenge you face is too difficult for God to overcome victoriously. Yet, ironically, ministers frequently quit in despair over their circumstances. Pastors resign because they dislike how they are being treated. One of the important effects prayer has on us is that it keeps us in a proper posture of surrender before our Lord.

Isaiah entered the temple filled with ideas about what God should do for his nation. But once He saw God sitting upon His heavenly throne, all the prophet could do was cry out *"Woe is me!"* and offer himself in humble service, saying, *"Here am I, send me!"* (Is. 6:5, 8).

Sin causes us to be self-centered. It fills us with pride and convinces us that we should not have to experience discomfort. But when we see our Lord as He is, we will undertake whatever task He gives us and meekly declare, *"We are unprofitable servants. We have done what was our duty to do"* (Lk. 17:10).

Nothing is impossible for God. But at times we become disoriented to Him, so we resist His work in our life. Not understanding His will or trusting His heart, we begin making demands of Him. We may refuse to serve Him in a difficult place or to endure suffering as a part of His will.

We met an associate pastor at a conference who told us the senior pastor of his church had recently retired. This man was convinced he should become the next senior pastor. We asked him how he would respond if the congregation called someone else to that role. He said he would immediately leave the church. He explained that, although God had called him to that church, he could not stay if they rejected him for a position he thought he deserved. Here was someone who was saying prayers, but who had not seen his Lord clearly. Certainly, the Son of God did not deserve the treatment He received at the hands of the ones He came to save, yet He humbly embraced His Father's will (Phil. 2:5-8). Jesus settled His posture of surrender in the Garden of Gethsemane when He prayed, *"Oh My Father, if it is possible, let this cup pass from Me; nevertheless, not as I will, but as You will"* (Matt. 26:39). Jesus clearly had no desire to be scourged and crucified. Such treatment was horrifically cruel and unjust. Nevertheless, it was necessary for the Father's will to be accomplished. There, in that sacred garden, the Son surrendered His pride, comfort, sense of fairness, and fears to His Father. Having surrendered His will in prayer, Jesus was fully prepared to go to the cross for the sins of humanity.

We often prefer commitments to acts of surrender. A commitment is something we do. Surrender is something God does. Commitment indicates we are in control. Surrender acknowledges we are powerless to achieve victory over our circumstances. We cannot experience success in our own strength and wisdom. We must surrender every area of our life to Christ so He can do in and through us what He alone can accomplish.

One area we desperately need to surrender to Christ is our holiness. Our pride seeks to make excuses for our sin. We were under a lot of stress . . . we were tired . . . we had a bad day . . . we deserve it. But as we pray, we accept God's evaluation of our sin and humbly repent of it. We may also need to surrender our unforgiving spirit. Many ministers have held on to resentment toward those who wounded or betrayed them. In prayer, we surrender those hurts and grievances to our Lord and acknowledge that we have no right to choose who we will and will not forgive. We may also need to surrender our sense of entitlement. Our pride can convince us that we deserve more recognition or a position or a certain level of pay and benefits. But in prayer, we release our rights to our Lord and acknowledge that it is our undeserved privilege to serve Him in any capacity. Regularly meeting with God and surrendering everything to Him allows us to remain unencumbered when He chooses to grant us our next assignment.

Prayer and Difficult Assignments

I (Richard) grew up in the home of a praying pastor. My father, Henry Blackaby, rose early every morning to meet with his Lord. Having surrendered his life fully to Christ, my father was prepared to make any sacrifice God asked of him. When I was eight, my parents informed us children that God was calling our family to relocate from southern California to Saskatoon, Saskatchewan, Canada. A small church was on the verge of disbanding there, and it had called my dad to be its pastor.

As a child, I couldn't understand why my father would leave a great church in California to go to a congregation of only ten people in Canada. In Saskatoon, I watched my father preach powerful sermons each week to a handful of people, yet the results were meager in the early days. One day I told my mother, "It doesn't seem right. Dad preaches such good sermons every week and yet no one responds. Hardly anyone comes to our church. I feel sorry for dad."

Unbeknownst to me, my mother alerted my father that his oldest son was struggling. Later that day, my dad took me aside. He assured me that he considered it an undeserved privilege to serve God in any place, among any people, under any condition. He told me I didn't need to feel sorry for him, because he was having the time of his life serving God. In truth, life was exceedingly difficult for our family in those days. Money was scarce, while criticism was abundant. Yet my father rose early every morning to meet with his Lord. There, in the still, quiet moments of the morning, my father surrendered to the Lord his desire for a new (or at least newer) car, home ownership, money to replace his threadbare suit, and relatives who lived less than 1,000 miles away.

Looking back on all God has done through my father over the years, I realize how much my father would have missed had he insisted on certain conditions for his service. Or if he had grown bitter because of the way people treated him. By surrendering his life afresh each day to his Lord, my father was in position to be of maximum service to his Master. As a result, God used him mightily.

6. Intercede for Others.

Ministers often feel more comfortable preaching to people than interceding on their behalf. Preaching is the highly public ministry pastors must perform each week. They know people will judge their performance as a minister largely on how they function in the pulpit. So, they labor all week to craft an interesting, creative sermon for Sunday.

When pastors preach, they speak to their congregation about God. But when they pray, they speak to God about their people. Neglecting prayer time to improve a sermon reveals a vain belief that preaching affects people more powerfully than prayer does. But as Spurgeon said, "There is no rhetoric like that of the heart, and no school for learning it but at the foot of the cross."[6] He also observed, "If we cannot prevail with men for God, we will at least, endeavor to prevail with God for men."[7] E.M. Bounds declared: "A prayerless ministry is the undertaker for all God's truth and for God's Church. He may have the most costly casket and the most beautiful flowers, but it is a funeral, notwithstanding the charmful array."[8]

The primary reason pastors neglect prayer is because they are not convinced it makes a tangible difference. If ministers truly believed their intercession moved heaven, they would spend many hours each day crying out to God

---

[6]Ibid., 44.
[7]Ibid., 45.
[8]Bounds, 106-107.

on their people's behalf. Instead, they proudly assume their sermons or Bible studies or opinions will exert a greater impact on people than will the working of the Holy Spirit as they pray.

Praying Against Evil

I (Richard) recall one evening when I was planning to take my wife out to celebrate our wedding anniversary. A deacon couple in our church had offered to care for our children that evening. As we dropped our children off at the couple's house, they alerted us that a married man was attempting to seduce one of the single moms in our church. That very evening, the church member was having the man over to her house for dinner. Our hearts broke. This woman had been trusting the Lord for her circumstances and was growing as a Christian. She knew what she was doing was wrong, but she had succumbed to the man's flattery and attention.

My wife and I had a miserable dinner! All we could think about was that a member of our church was toying with a sin that could destroy two families. We cut our evening short and returned to the deacon's home to retrieve our children. Sitting around their living room, we four adults prayed for the woman. We pleaded with God to convict her of the evil she was planning to commit before she went through with it.

When the man arrived at the woman's home, she felt so convicted about her sinful behavior that she refused to allow him inside. He pleaded to be allowed just a few minutes to talk with her, but she held firm and sent him away. I realized this woman had heard me preach each week, yet she had succumbed to temptation. However, as we prayed, the Spirit of God worked so powerfully in her life that she felt miserable until she turned from her wicked ways. My people needed more from their pastor than good preaching. They needed me to intercede on their behalf.

III. MODELING A LIFE OF PRAYER

The greatest influence pastors can exert on their people is not their preaching but their example. Ministers must live out their walk with God before their flock. As they do, people see the truth of their pastor's sermons incarnated in his life. Ministers must be careful, for Jesus warned that we should pray in secret and not use our prayer life as a means of boasting (Matt. 6:5). Nevertheless, wise ministers recognize that their example can exert a far more powerful effect for good than their words can. So, they use the example of their personal prayer life in a manner that inspires others to develop a prayer life of their own. The following are some practical ways ministers can use their prayer life to encourage their people.

First, let people know you pray. Guard yourself against using this disclosure as a means of self-promotion. Nevertheless, tell people that you pray for them. Refer to times God has ministered to you as you prayed. Share with your people the benefits you receive from time spent with God. People need to be reminded of the enormous benefits of prayer. They certainly need to know that their pastor is availing himself regularly of those rewards.

Second, send notes to people for whom you pray. Knowing your pastor is praying for you can bring enormous encouragement! Be specific! Let your people know exactly what you asked God to do in their lives. At times, God may fill your heart with a sense of what He intends to do in the life of one of your people. Perhaps you pray for a teenager who is faithfully living out her Christian faith at school. Or for a young father who is striving to be the man of God his wife and children need him to be. After you pray for them, take a moment to write them a note to let them know what you sense God has in His heart for them. As often as you can, cite the particular Scripture you are praying will become a reality in their life. Your notes to your members may become treasured keepsakes.

Third, invite others to join you in prayer. Whether they are making an evangelistic call, a hospital visit, or praying for the sick, prudent ministers invite others to join them whenever possible. Ministers can model for their members what interceding for others looks like. As people hear their pastor cry out to God, they will learn how they too can address their heavenly Father on behalf of others. Pastors can use these times to offer suggestions and encouragement to their congregants as they endeavor to become people of prayer.

Fourth, ministers ought to share answers to prayer with their people regularly and exuberantly. Nothing encourages prayer in the church more than hearing regularly of heaven's answers. Pastors who quickly give glory to God for His activity clearly demonstrate that they are not taking credit for the church's success. Such pastors know that the timely provision for their church's needs came from a loving, heavenly Father, not from their own administrative acumen or problem-solving abilities.

A Pastor's Prayer

God placed a burden in my (Rick) heart that our church should become a global missions sending center. Out of that burden was birthed an annual Global Missions Conference where we invited local, national, and international missionaries to minister to our congregation over several days. As we approached the first conference, I asked God to reveal where He wanted to use our church to make a difference globally.

On the first night of the conference, the missionaries serving in international settings dressed in the traditional attire of the people group they served. As one couple dressed in bright red national garb stood and introduced themselves, God spoke clearly to me, "Those are the people to whom I am calling this congregation." My heart was stirred and I could not wait to see how God orchestrated the connection. Through introductions and additional conversations, it became clear these were the people we were to pursue as our international mission focus.

After I shared with our church missions leadership team what God had said to me, they unanimously agreed that we should share this news with the congregation. What a joy for me to stand and celebrate where God was at work. The congregation enthusiastically embraced the vision God had given to me and the leadership team. More than 15 years later, even though I am no longer the pastor, the church is still deeply engaged in supporting God's work in that particular region. God spoke, we listened, and together we responded in obedience.

Fifth, pastors ought to develop a prayer culture in their church. Jesus said, *"It is written, My house will be called a house of prayer"* (Matt. 21:13). Nevertheless, although Jesus declared that prayer would be the defining characteristic of His house, prayer is only given a token role in many churches. For example, in a typical seventy-five-minute worship service, less than five minutes might be devoted to prayer. In a church business meeting or staff meeting, the meeting commences and ends in prayer, while everything in between is typically a compilation of the congregants' thoughts. Most church meetings are characterized by preaching, teaching, and arguing, but rarely by prayer.

Can you imagine the surprise if, during a church business meeting, the pastor devoted most of the time to prayer? Can you imagine the shock if a pastor told his staff that the church was facing so many challenges that they were going to devote their entire meeting to prayer? Can you imagine what people would think if, in response to the problem they were experiencing, the pastor immediately bowed his head and began praying for the need right there in the lobby? How radically would your church need to change for it to become known as a house of prayer?

Praying Before Deciding

I (Richard) was once a part of a church led by my brother Mel, who is a praying pastor. We needed to hire a new worship pastor. Of course, that endeavor has the potential to be extremely divisive. I remember the pastor making an announcement one Sunday morning about the process the church would follow. He announced that in two weeks, the church would hold a special business meeting on the matter. For the two weeks prior, however, the pastor charged the members with a special assignment. They were to take specific time to pray every day, seeking God's mind concerning our next worship pastor. Two weeks later at the business meeting, he would ask people to share, not what they thought, but what they heard from God as they prayed. But, the pastor cautioned, if any church member failed to pray each day about the matter, though they were welcome to attend the business meeting, they should refrain from comment. For the church was not interested in what people thought, but what God willed. If someone had not taken the issue seriously enough to pray about it, the church did not want to hear what that person had to say!

Not every pastor has the luxury of dealing with his church in this manner. But this pastor demonstrated that prayer was important in his church. In what ways are you as a leader showing that your church is a house of prayer?

CONCLUSION

Powerful, praying pastors lead powerful, praying churches. One does not go without the other. If you yearn for your church to pray in a manner that moves heaven and glorifies Christ, determine to move your prayer life from where it is to where God wants it to be. Refuse to accept any excuse for why you are not praying as you should. Tolerate no further delays. Clear your calendar, rise early, and stay in the place of prayer as long as necessary until the glory of God falls upon your congregation.

QUESTIONS FOR CONSIDERATION

1. On a scale of 1 to 10, with 10 being the highest, how would you currently rate your personal prayer life? How would your congregation rate it? How would God rate it?

2. What are the three greatest hindrances you face in prayer? What specific steps will you take to address them?

3. How many minutes during a typical worship service in your church is devoted to prayer? Is that adequate? Does that qualify as a "house of prayer"?

4. How does your personal prayer life encourage people in your church to pray? How often do people ask you to teach them how to pray?

5. What are three "takeaways" you believe God wants you to process from this chapter?

CHAPTER TWO

Praying Like Jesus

INTRODUCTION

If pastors want to minister like Jesus, they must learn to pray like Him. This feat is much easier said than done. Yet Jesus offered a glimpse into His prayer life that can serve as a template for our own.

John 17 records one of the most profound prayers ever documented: Jesus' prayer on the night He was arrested. In this prayer, Jesus revealed His profound love for His disciples. Even as the horror of the cross loomed before Him, Jesus' concern was for those He led. Jesus never wasted a word. He knew what was important. He was well aware of what lay in heaven's storehouse. So, He prayed in a focused, confident, specific fashion. In this chapter, we examine how Jesus prayed for those in His ministry. Pastors and church leaders should be praying in the same manner for those God has entrusted to their care.

I. THE HIGH PRIESTLY PRAYER OF JESUS

> *v1. "Jesus spoke these things, looked up to heaven, and said: 'Father, the hour has come. Glorify Your Son so that the Son may glorify You.'"*

Jesus prayed, *"the hour has come."* He always had an exquisite sense of heavenly timing. Prayer kept Jesus in sync with His Father's timetable. Jesus understood that it was not only important to act in the right *way*, but also at the right *time*. Jesus knew what His Father's will was, but He patiently waited on His Father's timing. Prayer helps pastors not only know *what* to do, but *when* to do it. It enables them to wait, sometimes for years, until God chooses to act.

Then Jesus prayed for something unusual. *"Glorify Your Son so that the Son may glorify You."* We are innately uncomfortable praying for God to glorify *us*. Such a request seems presumptuous. At first glance, it appears to be a prayer only the Son of God would dare utter. But synonyms for "glorify" are "magnify, lift up, exalt, make large." Jesus would soon be "lifted up" on a cruel cross. Yet He prayed not for His comfort or deliverance, but that those who saw Him on the cross would think more highly of His Father. Jesus was essentially saying, "Lord, place a magnifying glass over Me. When people look at Me closely, may they be impressed with You."

Pastor, whether you like it or not, your life is on constant display before your people. Rather than resent your lack of privacy, pray as Jesus did. Ask that when you suffer, your response points onlookers toward your heavenly Father. Living a comfortable life before others is easy. Living in a way that inspires others to join you despite your hardships is much more difficult. May it be true of you as it was of Jesus that as people examine your life, God is magnified.

v2. "for You gave Him authority over all flesh; so He may give eternal life to all You have given Him."
Jesus clearly understood the source of His authority. It was not His own; it had been granted to Him by His heavenly Father. As Jesus remained in communion with His Father, He had enormous spiritual power at His disposal. Wherever He exercised it, people were set free. The minister's spiritual authority comes, not from his position, but from his communion.

v3. "This is eternal life: that they may know You, the only true God, and the One You have sent, Jesus Christ."
Jesus understood that Christianity is not a religion. It is a relationship with the Father and Son through the Holy Spirit. Jesus did not focus on accumulating crowds of adherents, but on helping people enter into a life-changing, personal, obedient relationship with God. Pastors should not measure their success by the

size of their congregation, but by how intimately and passionately their people walk with God.

v4. *"I have glorified You on the earth by completing the work You gave Me to do."*

Jesus glorified God by completing every assignment His Father gave Him. As Jesus prayed for His disciples, He constantly asked, "Have I finished the work in their lives that You told me to begin?" Pastor, your job is not complete after you deliver a sermon on godly living. You must walk with your flock, pray for them, encourage and disciple them until they are practicing everything Jesus commanded (Matt. 18:20). Pastors must not leave their current place of ministry until they can say, as Jesus did, *"I have finished the work You gave Me to do."* Pray that it will be so!

v6. *"I have revealed Your name to the men You gave Me from the world. They were Yours, You gave them to Me . . ."*

In Jesus' culture, a person's name represented his character or nature. Jesus knew His behavior would determine what His disciples understood of God the Father. Likewise, pastors must remember that their actions influence people's view of God. If they constantly worry and fret about the problems they face, they portray God as a frail, unimpressive deity. If pastors speak of God as if He is merely a friend and not their Lord and Creator, they represent God as weak and insufficient.

Pastors must ask this question: Based on how I relate to God before my people, what can they conclude about God's nature?

One of the best ways to reflect God's true character to others is through public prayer. When you reverently pause to collect your thoughts before praying, you indicate that one should not carelessly rush into God's presence. When you speak reverently, humbly, and thoughtfully, you convey that God is far mightier and stronger than you are. When you earnestly repent of your sins, you clearly reveal God's holiness. When you pray sincerely, with genuine thoughts rather than shallow clichés, you depict God as personal, not merely a nebulous spiritual force. When you direct your words to God rather than to the audience, you demonstrate God's palpable presence. You must be careful, as Jesus was, to present God's name, or character, accurately to others.

Jesus noted that His disciples were a gift from the Father. As frustrating as Peter could be, the Father had given him to Jesus. Thomas was prone to doubt, but the Father had entrusted him to Jesus. The Father had even given Judas to His Son. Pastors should not grow impatient or hostile toward the people God has assigned to them! Prayer reminds pastors that their flock has been entrusted to them by God.

Jesus also recognized that His disciples originated from the world. They had spent most of their lives in a society with values and methods that were entirely foreign to God's. That is why James and John sought to outmaneuver their fellow disciples and gain the most coveted positions in Jesus' kingdom (Mark 10:35). That is also why the disciples argued over which of them was the greatest (Lk. 22:24). Jesus was not caught by surprise when His disciples acted like the world, because they had come from it. Much of a pastor's praying will be for the Holy Spirit to make their people less like the world and more like Christ.

> *v7. "Now they know that all things You have given Me are from You, v8. because the words that You gave Me, I have given them . . ."*

People can detect the source of our words. They can discern if we are motivated by pride, jealousy, or anger. They can also recognize if what we say originates from God. Jesus prayed that everything He spoke to His disciples would come directly from His Father. The fact that preachers cite a biblical text does not entail that God is the sermon's author. To determine the source of our words, we must examine their fruit. God's words set people free (John 8:32). Having people "enjoy" your sermon is inconsequential if none of them are freed by it! God's words always accomplish their purpose (Is. 55:10-11). It is not enough that your people claim to believe God's word; it must change them! Pastors ought to pray regularly that their sermons, teaching, and counsel come straight from heaven. Their people should expect nothing less.

*v9. "I pray for them. I am not praying for the world
but for those you have given Me, because they are
Yours."*

At this point, Jesus focused on the people His Father
had entrusted to Him. At times, pastors can become so
concerned about evangelizing unbelievers that they give
scant attention to the people God has already placed
in their congregation. Jesus understood that the key
to world evangelization is for the Church to function
the way God designed it. Jesus prayed for His disciples
because He understood that one church, functioning as
Christ intended, could impact an entire world. Pastor, do
your people know you are fervently praying to that end?

v11. "... so that they may be one as We are one."

Unity has always been challenging for God's people!
Even Jesus' twelve disciples experienced division. Jesus
constantly prayed that they would be one, just as the
Trinity is one. Jesus did not accept division. He did not
view unity as an unattainable goal. He continually prayed
that God would unite the hearts and minds of His people.
No pastor who regularly speaks with God will justify or
tolerate disunity in his congregation. A prayer-focused
pastor will earnestly intercede for his people and strive
to be a minister of reconciliation (2 Cor. 5:18).

v12. "While I was with them, I was protecting them by Your name that You have given Me. I guarded them and not one is lost, except the son of destruction, so that Scripture may be fulfilled."

Here we see Jesus as the Good Shepherd (Ps. 23). He regularly prayed that not one of the people God entrusted to Him would go astray. Sometimes pastors lose people too flippantly. At times, people leave the church angrily, blaming the pastor for their departure. On such occasions, pastors may be tempted to mutter "good riddance!" and rejoice that a "troublemaker" has departed. But shepherds with Jesus' heart cannot let someone go so easily. They grieve over every lost sheep. When members fall into sin or walk away from the church, godly pastors pray earnestly for their return. They do everything possible to restore their relationships. Shepherds who have Jesus' heart for their flock will strive to be able to declare, *"not one is lost."*

v13. "... I speak these things in the world so that they may have My joy completed in them."

Jesus knew that overflowing joy was an indication that someone was in a right relationship with Him (Jn. 15:11). He had to guard His own joy so He could share it with others. Would you wish your level of joy on your people? Is your church a joyful place? Does laughter reverberate down the hallways? Do children happily run into their Sunday School classrooms? Are your deacon and business meetings joyful occasions? Does your congregation have a reputation in the community for being joyful? Have you regularly prayed that it would be so?

v14. "I have given them Your word. The world hated them because they are not of the world."

Jesus only spoke words to His disciples that originated from heaven. But Jesus also knew that if His disciples embraced God's word, the world would hate them. This reality is sobering for today's pastors. Preachers face enormous pressure to make God's word palatable and attractive, not only to church members, but also to their church's community. Most pastors have no desire for their church to be a lightning rod for public contempt. Pastors typically avoid making statements from the pulpit that will upset congregants or cause people to leave the church. For this reason, pastors must pray that their people will hold firmly to God's word and that the Holy Spirit will protect them from a world that hates God's truth. For if your people live their lives based on God's word, they will inevitably face criticism, opposition, and scorn.

v15. "I am not praying that You take them out of the world but that You protect them from the evil one. v16. They are not of the world as I am not of the world."

Jesus was keenly aware that His followers were functioning in a foreign and hostile land. Satan and his evil minions hold much of the earth in their sinister grasp.

Darkness continually strives to snuff out the light (Jn. 1:5). Yet Jesus did not attempt to hide His people from the world or isolate them from its corrupting influence. Rather, Jesus intended to scatter His people throughout the earth as salt and light (Matt. 5:13-16). Jesus knew this plan was dangerous. In fact, He understood that His disciples would be criticized, opposed, arrested, and killed for His sake. So, He fervently prayed for God's protection.

The Christian life is not spent solely at church. Caring pastors pray for their people's protection as they enter the darkest corners of society every week. Conscientious pastors visit their people at their workplaces and homes so they can better understand the spiritual environment in which their congregants live. Loving pastors might prayer walk through their people's factories, hospitals, schools, and office buildings, calling on God for their flock's protection and courage. How blessed are people whose pastor earnestly prays on their behalf!

v17. "Sanctify them by the truth; Your word is truth."
Jesus understood that the key to His disciples' effectiveness was the degree to which they resembled Him. Jesus' focus was always on being, rather than doing. He prayed that His disciples would be sanctified. That is, that they would become like Him. Jesus' method was to expose them to God's word regularly. Scripture indicates that *". . . Christ loved the church and gave Himself for her, to make her holy, cleansing her in the washing of*

water by the word. He did this to present the church to Himself in splendor, without spot or wrinkle or any such thing, but holy and blameless" (Eph. 5:25-27). Pastors should constantly pray that God would use His word to sanctify their people. A pastor's opinions and viewpoints will not sanctify anyone. God's word will!

v18. "As You have sent Me into the world, I also have sent them into the world."

Jesus' goal was to prepare His disciples for their mission. Once He had sanctified them, He dispatched them throughout the world to make disciples of all nations. Many pastors focus on gathering people. They hate to lose anyone. But Jesus prayed that His Father would disperse His disciples globally. Pastors ought to pray regularly for the Lord of the harvest to thrust forth His people into the mission field. Pastors should not be surprised when members of their flock acknowledge that God is calling them to missions. A church without missionaries is a congregation that is not being prayed over as Jesus prayed for His disciples.

v19. "I sanctify Myself for them, so they also may be sanctified by the truth."

Our self-management is the key to our ministry. Jesus ministered out of the overflow of His own walk with the Father. He asked nothing of His disciples that He did not do Himself.

Pastors ought to be keenly aware that their example will either be a stepping stone or a stumbling block to their people's godliness. Jesus claimed that He sanctified Himself so His people could be sanctified. Pastors cannot afford to allow pride into their heart, for it could cause their people to stumble. Pastors cannot cling to bitterness or unforgiveness, for it could prove too costly for their flock. Pastors must regularly pray, as David, that God would search their heart and root out any unclean thing from their life (Ps. 139:23-24).

This one prayer does not constitute Jesus' entire prayer life, but we can see from these selected verses the nature and focus of His intercession. Can you imagine having a pastor who prayed for you in this manner? Jesus' prayer is focused and intentional. It is God-centered. It runs deep. Our hope is that you would allow God to take your prayer life to these sacred depths. Your people are counting on it.

II. PRACTICAL STEPS TO DEEPENING YOUR PRAYER LIFE

Numerous pastors have asked us what practical steps they can take to deepen their prayer life. Often these sincere ministers recognize that their prayer life is woefully inadequate, but they don't know how to strengthen it. The following are some simple suggestions.

1. Study the Prayers in the Bible.

The Bible is filled with powerful, God-honoring prayers. Set aside time to examine how people like Abraham, Moses, Hannah, Elijah, Daniel, Nehemiah, Ezra, and Paul prayed. Carefully study each of Jesus' prayers. Notice their passion. Take note of their confidence in God, as well as their personal humility in His presence. Heed their confession of sin. Consider their requests. Observe their posture before God.

Then take time to pray those same prayers for your people. Use some of the same phrases. Pray about identical issues. Infuse your prayers with Scriptural content. Proverbs 13:20 assures us that we will become like the people with whom we spend time. Invest frequent time with the great intercessors of the Bible and allow them to dramatically affect your prayer life.

2. Study God's Nature and Character

Take time to do an extensive study of God's attributes. For example, study God's holiness in depth. In light of God's holiness, what sins are exposed in your life? How do you need God to forgive and consecrate you? How then should you pray for your people's holiness? Study God's power. Is your ministry characterized by the awesome power of God? If not, what is impeding God's might in your life and church? Ask God to remove anything hindering His work in and through your life. Examine God's joy. How does it compare with yours? If you are not experiencing God's fullness of joy, prayerfully seek the reason. Stay with God in prayer until He removes any barriers to His joy in your life (John 15:11). Study God's heart. Notice His love for the outcast, for sinners, for the poor. Then prayerfully ask God if you love what He loves and hate what He hates. Once again, allow God to reveal areas in your life where you are not in sync with His heart. Continue this process with each of God's character traits. We can assure you that this exercise will dramatically deepen your prayer life!

3. Study What Scripture Says About Prayer

Carefully take inventory of your prayer life to be sure it is perfectly aligned with what Scripture teaches. For example, Matthew 7:7 says, *"Keep asking, and it will be given. Keep searching, and you will find. Keep knocking, and the door will be opened to you."* This teaching is straightforward. If we keep asking, we will receive. We must ask, Have I continued to ask? Have I received? Or have I grown weary in asking? We ought to record our requests in a prayer journal, then review what we have received. If we have not received answers to our prayers, we ought to be gravely concerned. Continuing to pray in the same fruitless manner is foolhardy.

In Matthew 17:20, Jesus told His disciples, *". . . For I assure you: If you have faith the size of a mustard seed, you will tell this mountain, 'Move from here to there,' and it will move. Nothing will be impossible for you."* Again, we must hold our prayer life accountable to this verse. Jesus said *nothing* would be impossible to those who believed. Are spiritual mountains moving because of our prayers? Do we pray as if nothing is impossible? If we truly believed nothing was impossible when we prayed, would we not pray more often? Do the people who listen to you sense that you believe you can move mountains when you pray?

One final example is found in Jeremiah 33:3. God invited His people, *"Call to Me and I will answer you and tell you great and wondrous things you do not know."* Once again, we must ask ourselves, "Have I been calling to God and asking for His guidance? Has He revealed things to me that I did not know?" In our prayer journal, we ought to list the questions we have asked God, and beside them, we should list the answers He has provided. Too often we see God's promises in Scripture but never avail ourselves of them. Or we pray, but then fail to hold ourselves accountable for any results.

Numerous statements and promises about prayer are imbedded throughout Scripture. Take time to systematically lay your life and ministry next to each one. Stay focused on those truths until each one is an active, practical reality in your life.

4. Pray for Spiritual Discernment.

The apostle Paul prayed, *"I pray that you . . . may be able to comprehend with all the saints what is the length and width and height and depth of God's love, and to know the Messiah's love that surpasses all knowledge, so you may be filled with all the fullness of God."*

What an awesome prayer! How incredible it would be to comprehend the length, width, height, and depth of God's love that surpasses all knowledge. How would such knowledge affect our ministry? If we truly understood the depth of God's love for us, would we worry about our problems? Would we struggle to make time to pray? How would such knowledge affect the way we pray for people? How would it impact the way we treat others? How would it influence the way we respond to our enemies?

Often when we meet pastors who are discouraged or burned out, we find people who do not fully grasp God's love. They may understand it intellectually, but not experientially. As a result, pastors may struggle to comprehend many issues, such as godly church members' suffering or the working of evil in the world. Pastors can be tempted to zero in on the physical issues and miss the deeper, spiritual causes. Take time to pray for spiritual understanding of the deep issues of God. Don't assume that believing a doctrine means you are actually practicing and experiencing that truth in your life and ministry!

5. Read the Prayers of the Saints.

One final exercise to deepen your prayer life is to immerse yourself, not only in the prayers of Scripture, but also in the prayers of history's greatest prayer warriors. Men such as E.M. Bounds, Charles Spurgeon, George Muller and many others provide compelling examples of prayer. A helpful volume we have used is *The*

Valley of Vision, which is a collection of Puritan prayers and devotions. Reading the prayers of the saints can be a deeply energizing experience. Immerse yourself in deep, fervent, biblically-based, mountain-moving prayer. You must develop this discipline, for reading other people's prayers can be difficult. But hold your own prayers next to theirs. Notice the depth of their requests. Observe the reverence with which they address the Lord. Watch for the type of requests they choose to make on behalf of others. Anyone can become complacent if they compare themselves with slothful people. If a pastor compares his prayer life with an ordinary church member, he may feel superior in many respects in his devotional life. Holding our prayers next to the greatest saints is far better. The point of this exercise is not to berate ourselves but to acknowledge the many heights of prayer to which we have yet to ascend! Such reading should inspire us never to become satisfied until we have grown our prayer life to a level that pleases the God of our prayers.

This list is far from exhaustive. It simply offers a few suggestions of how to move from where your prayer life is toward where God wants it to be. Be satisfied with nothing less than the fullness of God's power every time you pray. Others will suffer if your prayer life falls short of what it could be.

III. A PRAYER GUIDE

Pastors have access to numerous conferences and books on prayer. We have found that a practice as crucial as prayer can easily become so entangled by numerous approaches and methods that those "helps" inadvertently become distractions. Below is a simple, practical guide that has helped many people as they sought to simultaneously enrich and simplify their prayer life. This is certainly not the only approach, but it has proven effective for many who have used it. We hope it encourages you!

A Guide for Personal Prayer

WORSHIP: Begin the prayer time with worship, using a Psalm or other passage of scripture. Identify, underline, and write down everything the passage reveals about God. Then praise God for those specific truths. This practice can transform your view of God and enrich your relationship with Him.

GRATITUDE: In that same passage, identify truths for which you are thankful. Spend time counting His gracious gifts, naming them one by one. This practice cultivates a grateful heart that learns to identify God's blessings and activity.

REPENTANCE: Next, ask God to search your heart (Ps. 139:23-24) for sin. Praying Psalm 51:10 and 1 John 1:9, ask Him to cleanse you from all unrighteousness and to create in you a clean and pure heart. Do not rush this step! You will not experience

God's forgiveness and cleansing unless you have identified your sin (from God's perspective), and repented of it.

LISTEN: Now you are ready to hear clearly from Him through other scripture passages or devotional material.

ASKING: Your heart is prepared and oriented to know what to ask of God, whether for yourself or on behalf of someone else

CONCLUSION

This chapter is designed to start moving your prayer life in the right direction. Too much is at stake merely to continue praying in the same manner we have in the past. We have listed a select bibliography on prayer at the end of this book. Those resources can enrich your prayer life if you avail yourself of them. Ask the Lord what steps you need to take so your prayer life begins moving into the deep waters of God's heart and activity. Then immediately take practical steps to implement what God says!

QUESTIONS FOR CONSIDERATION

1. As you read John chapter 17, in what ways do your prayers resemble Jesus' prayer? In what

ways are you currently neglecting to pray as Jesus prayed?

2. Would you wish your current level of joy on your congregation? How might God increase your joy?

3. Have you properly sanctified yourself on behalf of your people? How might you increase the level of your holiness?

4. What is the current pattern you use in your private devotional life? Do you need to adjust it? Are there some ways you can refresh your time with God and invigorate your prayer life?

5. What is one adjustment you intend to make immediately in the way you pray and spend time with your Lord?

CHAPTER THREE

Leading Your Church to Pray

INTRODUCTION

Before pastors can lead their churches to pray, they must cultivate their personal prayer life. Once they have done so, church leaders can take many practical steps to develop the prayer culture in their church. In the following pages, we suggest numerous ways pastors can guide their people to become a praying congregation. However, we offer one caution: Let God guide you. Don't merely copy what you find in this book or what appears to be successful in another church. God has unique assignments for each congregation. As a consequence, your church may incorporate different prayer ministries than a sister church does.

The following are several ways God may guide ministers as they help their congregation develop into a powerful, praying church.

PULPIT MINISTRY

Pastors have the unparalleled opportunity to teach, exhort, and inspire their flock concerning prayer. A pastor's pulpit ministry can exert enormous impact when done properly. The following are some of the most important ways pastors can utilize the pulpit to promote prayer among their people.

A. Pulpit Praying

For many pastors, the highlight of their weekly ministry is when they stand behind the pulpit and exhort their people from God's word. But preaching is not the only ministry that takes place from the sacred desk.

Charles Spurgeon often said that if he had to choose between preaching and praying in a worship service, he would choose to pray. D.L. Moody once visited the famous Metropolitan Tabernacle in London. When someone later asked what he thought of Spurgeon's preaching, Moody exclaimed that it was excellent. However, what impressed him most was Spurgeon's praying. On many occasions, people attended services at the Tabernacle to hear the great orator speak, but they came away inspired by his prayers.

B. Modeling Prayer

Today's worship services generally include public prayers, but these are often trite, cliché-riddled utterances used as transitions between various segments of the worship service.

Cliché Praying

During the morning service at a church I (Richard) visited, the worship leader prayed four times. All four prayers were nearly identical. While the worship leader prayed the first time, his worship team took their places on stage. During his second prayer, the pastor entered the baptistry. During his third prayer, the worship team left the stage. After his fourth prayer, the congregation was dismissed. No one experienced a sense of reverence or awe as the worship leader led the people into God's holy presence. Everyone knew he was simply utilizing a technique for moving people back and forth on stage while everyone's eyes were closed. He used the same clichés repeatedly. He employed a familiar vernacular that sounded more appropriate for a conversation between two friends watching a football game than a worshipper entering the awesome presence of almighty God.

While many of today's pastors are careless in their public praying, others have excised the pastoral prayer altogether. Pastors would never consider eliminating the sermon from the worship service, but many churches have discarded the pastoral prayer. This omission is a travesty, for it is the only proper, God-honoring prayer many people experience all week. Pastors ought to diligently guard their opportunity to pray for their people during the worship service. The congregation needs to see what genuine, biblical, passionate, faith-filled prayers look, sound, and feel like.

Pastors often lament that their people do not pray as they should. Yet the pastor's own prayers may be part of the problem. For the average churchgoer, the people they hear pray more often than any others are the leaders of their church. The prayers pronounced during worship services set the standard for how Christians view prayer. Before leveling a charge against their prayerless congregants, pastors do well to ask, "After hearing me pray from the pulpit each week, why do my people have no interest in prayer?"

We might expect the twelve disciples to ask Jesus to teach them to preach, walk on water, feed multitudes, or raise the dead. But their only request for instruction recorded in Scripture was when they asked Jesus to teach them to pray (Lk. 11:1). We can conclude that after hearing Jesus talk to His Father, the twelve longed to speak to God in a similar manner.

Pastors should consider how often their prayers impact their flock so strongly they long to pray in a similar manner. We do not pray to impress. But clearly Jesus' prayers deeply effected those who heard them. The following are some considerations for public prayer:

• *Designate appropriate time* in the service, or in church meetings, for prayer. Don't dishonor God with a rushed, brief moment specifically allotted to talking to Him. Many churches today devote less than five minutes of an hour-long service to prayer. Jesus said His Father's house was to be a place of prayer. Yet at times, singing one chorus takes more time than all the prayers of the service combined.

• *Prepare your thoughts.* Some pastors believe preparing a prayer in advance is unspiritual. But in truth, doing so is entirely appropriate. If you were given the opportunity to address the president of the United States, you would carefully think through what to say. You would not waste time with redundancy. You would not offer threadbare clichés. You might not read a manuscript verbatim, but you would certainly outline your thoughts to ensure you addressed important topics thoroughly and thoughtfully.

There is nothing innately "spiritual" about being unprepared when speaking to almighty God! Pastors must understand that the way they address

God from the pulpit becomes a model for how their people pray in private. Pastors must also realize that their people listen to them pray each week and do not want to hear the same prayer every time. Instead, pastors ought to address a wide range of issues in their prayers. On Thanksgiving Sunday, pastors might express gratitude to God. On Easter, they might focus on the power and implications of the resurrection. On Mother's Day, pastors can ask for a blessing on mothers. Each week, the pastor's prayer should focus on his people's needs and the issues they currently face.

Pastors might also concentrate their prayers on God's attributes. One week the pastor might pray about God's power and how the church desperately needs it. The next week the pastor might pray about God's patience, love, and forgiveness and how the people need to experience each one. The pastor might address various ways God works in people's lives. One week he might focus on conviction of sin. The following weeks he might pray for God to protect his people from harm or provide for their needs.

Other times pastors might choose a Scripture verse and pray it word by word for their people. Pastors can lift up government leaders one week and area churches and ministries another week. Pastors can pray each Sunday for a different fruit of the Spirit to be manifested in their people's lives.

They can also pray specifically against sins that are present in their congregation. If pastors take time to prepare their thoughts in advance, their pulpit prayers can be biblically rich, topically diverse, and profoundly timely every week.

• *Choose Your Words Carefully.* Pastors should not only select the major themes for their prayers carefully, but also the specific words. For example, a common prayer in church services today is, "God, we ask you to be with us today." Of course, God is with you if you are a Christian. He promised He would be with us always (Matt. 28:20). What we should pray is, "Lord, open our spiritual eyes so we recognize Your presence in our midst today!" Another common prayer is this: "Lord, we invite you into our service today!" This statement implies that God is outside the auditorium door waiting for a formal invitation. The truth is, *we* are guests in *His* house! We need to draw near to Him (James 4:8).

Likewise, people who pray publicly need to be careful that their prayers are theologically correct. For example, don't pray: "And we know that You love us just the way we are!" For that statement is patently false. Holy God loves us *despite* the way we are! If He loved us just the way we are, He would not have sent His beloved Son to die on a cross for our sins! He is broken-hearted over our sinful state.

Furthermore, don't pray, "And Lord, we know you cannot use an unclean vessel!" Be cautious when declaring what God *cannot* do. God often *will not* do something, but that does not necessarily mean He *cannot*. God most assuredly prefers to use clean vessels for His work, but He does not restrict Himself to them. God used Nebuchadnezzar to punish Judah. He used Cyrus to allow the exiles to return to Jerusalem. God used the Roman legions to bring judgment on Jerusalem. These people were by no means holy vessels, but they were instruments in God's hand nonetheless.

Why is theological correctness important? Because public prayers are model prayers. When we make inaccurate or unbiblical statements, we disrespect God and mislead people. If pastors want to develop powerful praying churches, they must strive to provide the grandest examples possible of what God-honoring prayer looks like. They must be acutely conscious that careless statements from the pulpit may be repeated in their people's homes for years to come.

• *Prepare Your Heart.* God does not heed the prayers of those with sinful hearts (Prov. 15:29). Pastoral prayers may be eloquent and theologically laden, but if the pastor's heart is displeasing to God, his prayer will be stillborn (Is. 59:1-2). People want to be confident that when their pastor prays,

God listens. A pastor's walk with God is on display every time he prays publicly. Everyone heard what the pastor asked of heaven. Now they wait to see how God responds.

Another reason pastors must have pure hearts is because they cannot pray with power and passion when their hearts and minds are sinful. Passionless praying is an affront to almighty God. Yet many prayers offered in churches across the land today are lifeless, dull, and at times, painful to hear. Pastors should not utter boring prayers if they want to inspire their congregation to be fervent intercessors. People loved listening to Charles Spurgeon pray because his prayers were the most dynamic portion of the worship service. Sadly, in many churches today, the pastoral prayer has become so dull and lifeless that it has been discreetly replaced with seemingly more exciting alternatives.

When you pray, you are talking to the God who created the universe and will judge all of humanity. Pray with passion, conviction, and confidence.

Pastoral Pleading

Several years ago I (Richard) was the guest speaker at a church on a Sunday morning. When the time came for the pastoral prayer, the pastor surprised me. He stepped down from the platform and knelt. Rather than a dry, predictable, dispassionate monologue, he launched into agonized pleading with God on behalf of his people. I had never heard such heartfelt intercession for someone's church. It deeply moved me. I could not imagine how anyone in that congregation could doubt that their pastor loved them or that God would answer his prayers on their behalf. After hearing that man pray, I was inspired to pray differently myself.

PROTECT CORPORATE PRAYER TIMES.

Just as pastors must be careful how they pray before their people, they must also be protective of how others pray during the worship service. Churches often assign people to say public prayers, not because they are prayer warriors or people of profound faith, but because they hold a particular ecclesiastical office. If the chairman of the deacons or elder board is not a person of prayer, he should not be asked to pray publicly (And he should not be the chairman of the deacons or elders!). We ought always to be more concerned with honoring God than honoring people.

The largest donor in the church may be carnal or unspiritual. He should be passed over for public prayers, and a godly widow or a devout teenager asked to pray instead. Only put people before the congregation who can provide a healthy model for those who listen.

In many churches, one of the ushers prays before collecting the offering. Often, the ushers themselves choose who will pray. At times, these prayers can be God-dishonoring, boring, or even heretical. Pastors must beware that every time they present a poor example of public prayer, they discourage their people from praying themselves.

God-Dishonoring Offertory Praying

When I (Richard) was a college student, I was made the chairman of the ushers for my church. I took the responsibility seriously. I organized the ushers into teams. I appointed team captains. I scheduled monthly ushers meetings to address various concerns. But I received a shock during a worship service. Before the offering was collected, one of the ushers said the offertory prayer. It was the most theologically-inaccurate, boring prayer I had ever heard! This man obviously did not pray often, for he seemed completely clueless about how to speak to God.

I realized that I had focused on collecting the offering and distributing programs, but I had completely neglected the ushers' most important task: offering public prayer. During the next ushers meeting we addressed prayer. I emphasized that they were not reciting a dry liturgy; they were talking directly to God. I told them I did not want to hear them use Christian clichés. Rather, I wanted them to prepare in advance what they would ask God to do. When the time came, they were to speak reverently, lovingly, and thoughtfully about what was on their heart for the church. I also determined who prayed so those who were unprepared would not feel obligated to take a turn. In time, each person prayed. It was heartwarming to hear them speak to God in a manner that honored Him and blessed the people.

PULPIT PREACHING/TEACHING

Ministers can promote prayer among their congregation, not only by example, but also by their teaching and preaching.

1. Prayers of the Bible

Throughout the year, pastors should regularly reference prayer in their sermons. Pastors might present a series of messages on prayers in the Bible. Scripture contains a goldmine of truth about how to pray properly. The Lord's Prayer provides a wonderful model that pastors ought to teach often (Matt. 6:9-13). Jesus' high priestly prayer is a profound example of God-honoring prayer (John 17). Intercessory prayers by biblical giants such as Moses (Ex. 32:11-14; 30-35), Daniel (Daniel 9), and Ezra (Ezra 9) are rich in teaching material. The Apostle Paul's deeply theological prayers include rich insights into biblical praying (Eph. 1:15-23; 3:14-20; Col. 1:9-14).

The Bible also records the various ways God responds to prayer. Nehemiah continually prayed while he administered Jerusalem and rebuilt the wall. As a result, God protected him and granted him success. David frequently cried out to God for protection from his enemies and God repeatedly delivered him. Joshua prayed and the sun stood still! Jonah prayed from the belly of a great fish and God heard him. Elijah prayed and God sent fire from heaven. Scripture is filled with examples of what prevailing prayers of faith look like.

Numerous Bible verses speak directly to the nature of prayer. Jeremiah 33:3 instructs us to call on the Lord and He will answer us and show us great and mighty things which we do not know. Jesus promised that if we ask, we will receive. If we seek, we will find. If we knock, the door will be opened to us (Matt. 7:7). The apostle James assures us that the effective, fervent prayer of a righteous person avails much (James 5:16). Scripture also speaks concerning prayer for revival (2 Chr. 7:14). A pastor never needs to look far to find biblical material on prayer.

2. Testimonies of Answered Prayer.

A second way pastors can use pulpit ministry to promote prayer is by allowing people to share testimonies of answered prayer. Again, the pastor ought to monitor these testimonies carefully and provide clear instructions to those who speak. He might consider asking people to provide a manuscript of what they intend to say. Doing so can keep untrained speakers from going too long or getting off track. It is typically best to control the microphone as well in case the person sharing needs to be stopped or brought back on target.

Pastors need not fear having unprofessional speakers share from the pulpit. Many of the great revivals in history began when laypeople spoke about what God had done in their life. People expect their pastor to urge them to pray. Yet when the congregation hears how God worked powerfully in response to common church member's prayers, others may be inspired to pray as well.

3. Provide Opportunities to Pray.

If prayer is as important as the pastor claims, people ought to have ample opportunities to pray at church. The pastor can provide this opportunity in at least three different ways.

a) Prayer Meetings.

Weekly prayer meetings used to be customary for most churches. However, those gatherings have become so sparsely attended that few remain. Sadly, this neglect is often the result of the uninspiring prayer that occurred during the meetings. In truth, if you attend a prayer meeting today, the majority of the service is often spent on activities other than praying. The pastor may take half the time to lead in Bible study. Then a large amount of time is spent sharing prayer requests. In some prayer meetings, one or two deacons will pray on behalf of the people at the close of the service. Typically, very little time is devoted to praying.

Our challenge to you is this: if you have a prayer meeting, be sure you spend the bulk of the service praying! Do not take up much time sharing prayer requests. People often prefer talking about prayer to actually praying. Instead, have people quickly move into a time of prayer.

We have heard pastors confess that their people would stop attending the prayer meeting if they were asked to pray. Then so be it! Better to have a handful of people earnestly crying out to God than a room full of people hearing a devotional about prayer and then deluding themselves into thinking they are people of prayer.

b) Prayer During the Worship Service.

Ministers should never hesitate to invite people to pray during a worship service. After all, God said His house was to be a house of prayer (Matt. 21:13). The only time Jesus resorted to violence was when people were prevented from praying in the house of worship.

Calls to prayer can take many forms. Pastors may allow moments of silence during the service so people can pray where they are sitting. In my (Richard) church, there is a pastoral prayer every Sunday morning. During that time, the pastor invites people to come to the front of the auditorium to pray. The altar is always full of individuals, couples, and entire families who feel led to pray.

My (Rick) pastor recently called the congregation to an extended prayer time during a morning worship service. The pastor's sermon was on family issues. During this particular worship time, he invited us to approach the altar and join him in praying specifically for our families. He encouraged us not to be timid or feel awkward. Parents and grandparents seeking God's blessing for their families flooded the altar. For the next 15 minutes, the pastor led as we sought God together. What a powerful experience we had as God responded to His people's prayers for their families!

From time to time, special occasions will occur, such as a short-term mission trip or Vacation Bible School. Preceding these events, it may be appropriate to designate time during the service for people to pray over those who will be serving. Perhaps those going on a mission trip could stand across the front of the auditorium while people pray over them. My (Richard) father used to have the church pray over the schoolteachers in our congregation on the Sunday before school commenced for the year. Perhaps the adults could gather around the teenagers to pray for them before they leave for their youth mission trip. These commissioning times send a strong message to the congregation that the church believes in, and practices, prayer.

Praying for a Ministry Team

My (Rick) congregation assembled a ministry team charged with seeking God's guidance for how we should reach our community. Having selected the team, I brought them to the altar at the conclusion of worship. Then I invited the congregation to lay hands on the team members. I asked those who did not come forward to stretch out their hands and join me in prayer as we consecrated the team for this specific undertaking.

As the team began their work, we asked the congregation to pray for them each week. When the team later reported what they sensed God saying to them about our church's future, the congregation experienced great joy and unity. Undoubtedly, God used our corporate praying to bring harmony and willingness to pursue what He revealed.

Finally, the pastor can invite people to pray during the altar call. Too often pastors restrict the altar call to three specific people groups: those who need to pray to receive Christ, those who need to be baptized, and those who want to join the church. But people may need to come forward to pray for many reasons, and they should be welcomed.

Many churches have all but eliminated the altar call in worship services today. They worry that it puts too much pressure on people. Or, if no one "walks the aisle," it can cast the preacher and his sermon in an unfavorable light. So churches improvise by inviting people to fill out a card or to contact the church office during the week.

We believe it is important for people to respond to what they heard God say during the service. If someone just heard God speak, they need to take action immediately. At the close of the service, pastors should invite their people to come to a designated area in the auditorium to pray and commit themselves to obey what God said. Certainly we want people to experience salvation. But many people in the congregation are believers who have already been baptized and joined the church. Yet they may still need to respond to the sermon. If you challenge men on Father's Day to rise up and be spiritual leaders in their home, invite the men to come forward to pray at the close of the service. Or welcome wives to join their husbands at the altar to pray that their husbands would have victory over sin and become mighty men of God. If you preach on surrendering to God's will, invite people to come to the altar to release everything in their life to their Lord. Week after week, invite people to draw near to God in prayer at the close of the service. Have pastors or counselors available at the front of the auditorium to pray with those who come forward.

If you have not regularly offered an altar call, don't be disheartened if your congregants do not respond immediately. This practice will be foreign to them. They will need time to see the value of coming forward to pray.

At first, only a handful may come, but that is okay. We have found that once your church members begin to respond regularly to what God tells them in the service, a growing number of people will desire salvation and baptism as well.

Never minimize the effect it has on your congregation when someone comes to the altar to pray. We have heard some pastors belittle this time of response, arguing that what matters is what people do after they leave the service. They argue that if the sermon was about evangelism, people do not need to come to the altar to pray. The pastor should encourage them to leave the building and start witnessing! Indeed, some people would rather pray about obeying than obey. But in our experience, if someone leaves their seat, walks to the front, kneels, and commits to take an action, they are far more likely to follow through after they leave the auditorium. By asking people to come forward to pray during the altar call, you are creating a culture of response to God's word. You will find that when the altar is filled with people responding to God in prayer at the end of each service, many of those who came forward will carry through with those commitments throughout the weeks and years to come.

Time to Respond!

If you invite people to come forward to pray, be sure to provide adequate time for them to do so. I (Richard) remember speaking at an older, formal church several years ago. The pastor told me I could give an altar call at the close of the service. But he warned me that the people were not comfortable with that form of response, so few, if any, would respond. Nevertheless, the people seemed extremely attentive throughout my sermon, and I sensed God was speaking to many of them. At the close of the service, I invited people to come forward to pray. To my surprise, many people began making their way down the long aisles to the front of the auditorium. Congregants flooded the altar, and more people were making their way forward from the back of the auditorium. I nodded to the senior pastor to guide his people for the remainder of the response time. But to my dismay, the pastor immediately brought the music to a close and instructed the ushers to start collecting the morning offering. Because of the widespread response, the service was running late and he wanted to end on time! The altar call sputtered to an untimely end.

That evening, the pastor and I discussed what I had witnessed. I suggested that the issue was not that his people did not want to respond in prayer. Rather, the problem was that they were not given adequate time to do so. I told him the people did not feel "safe" coming to pray, because they would soon be stranded at the altar as the service moved on to the offertory. During the next service, I assured the congregation that we would leave plenty of time for people to pray before we concluded the service. A mass of people came forward! They clearly longed to do business with God. They just needed time to do so.

c) Special Prayer Times

Another way pastors can teach their people to pray is by holding special prayer times for specific purposes. The pastor might ask people to gather on Saturday or Sunday afternoon to pray for national revival or for an upcoming election. Some churches usher in the New Year with prayer.

Special Prayer Times

I (Richard) used to invite people to meet every Friday morning at 6:00 a.m. to pray specifically for the upcoming Sunday services. I recall one Friday morning when everyone in our prayer group sensed God was going to do something special the following Sunday. Sure enough, we experienced a record attendance. No special event was scheduled, but people inexplicitly kept pouring into our auditorium until the ushers had to scramble to find additional seating. My prayer warriors had known since Friday that something unusual was going to happen on Sunday.

The next Friday as we prayed, we once again sensed that something unusual was going to happen on Sunday. However, the attendance on Sunday was well below what it had been the previous week. We had been so certain God would do something significant, yet the service appeared to be ordinary. Then we extended the altar call. Suddenly, person after person stepped out into the aisle and made their way to the front to speak with a pastor. Numerous people asked to be baptized. Once again, my people sensed in prayer on Friday that God was going to work mightily on Sunday. Our Friday morning prayer times became exciting occasions for those who attended.

At one point, our church finances began lagging behind our expenses. We had undertaken some new ministries that stretched our budget. We believed we were obeying God's direction, but we were not receiving enough funds through our weekly offerings to cover the expenses.

The church's finance committee approached me and asked if they could hold a special day of prayer on a Saturday to focus on our church's financial need. They assembled various stations throughout the auditorium where people could pray. They set out information itemizing what God had led us to do and the finances we required. One station listed the exact amount of money we owedneeded to pay off the church's debt. Another station contained various scripture verses about giving and stewardship. The finance committee organized the entire prayer event.

Several significant things occurred shortly afterward. First, we took a special offering the following Sunday designated to eliminating the church's debt. Not surprisingly, we collected exactly what we owed. Second, a church in a distant state heard about what we were doing and felt led to help us. During the same week we took our own offering, a check for the exact amount of money we had needed arrived in the mail from the other church. After devoting a special day to pray for our finances, we suddenly had twice as much money as we required! We ultimately used the unexpected gift to pay off our church mortgage early, releasing funds in our monthly budget for new ministries God called us to undertake. Third, as a result of that experience, many church members made fresh commitments to the Lord regarding their personal giving. Some committed to begin tithing. Others increased their monthly donations. One focused day of prayer brought great blessing to our church!

Pastors can promote prayer among their people in various ways. Their wise use of the pulpit and other methods can pay rich dividends in their people's prayer lives.

DEVELOPING A PRAYER MINISTRY AND PRAYER MINISTRY LEADERSHIP TEAM

While pastors must have the vision and desire to lead their flock to become prayer warriors, our experience has been that pastors rarely have adequate time to lead the prayer ministry by themselves. If prayer is to be a foundational ministry of the church, pastors must enlist others to help. Churches with strong prayer ministries often have a Prayer Ministry Coordinator, a Prayer Ministry Leadership Team, and designated money in the church budget to develop and sustain the ministry.

The Prayer Ministry Coordinator, who will work closely with the pastor, should be the first person enlisted. Essential qualities for this leadership role are: (1) a passion for personal and corporate prayer; (2) a belief that God works through prayer; (3) a vision or "big picture" of the church as a house of prayer; (4) good communication and leadership skills.

In enlisting prayer ministry leadership, pastors must observe how God is working to develop individuals in their congregation into people of prayer. Perhaps certain church members have expressed interest in deepening their prayer life or in a specific area of prayer. These people could eventually become a part of the Prayer Ministry Leadership Team.

Roles of the Prayer Ministry Team:
The Prayer Ministry Leadership Team's key role is to assist the pastor in teaching, equipping, and mobilizing the congregation to pray. (See Appendix 1: organizational chart).

Teach and Equip
One of the Prayer Ministry's goals is to provide teaching for the congregation in biblical principles concerning personal and corporate prayer. Teaching methods include annual prayer conferences, special studies on prayer, and year-round discipleship classes. Additionally, The Prayer Ministry Team should make various tools and resources available to the congregation, such as biblical prayer guides on various topics and books on prayer. The Prayer Ministry can also assist in writing prayer guides for mission team members, as well as for those enlisted to pray for the mission trip.

Annual Prayer Conference
When I (Rick) was a pastor, our church organized an annual prayer conference. Each year we brought in an outstanding speaker to teach biblical principles of prayer. We made this event a financial priority. We also invited local churches to attend the conference so they could be encouraged in prayer as well.

Mobilize

Another role of the Prayer Ministry Team is to provide specific opportunities for church members to practice what they have learned about prayer in ways that align with their interests and passions. While not an exhaustive list, we have seen the following types of prayer ministry develop in various churches to great effect. Each prayer ministry should have a designated leader.

INTERCESSORY MINISTRY AND PRAYER ROOM

As part of an intercessory prayer ministry, church members make a one-year commitment to pray at a certain time each week in the prayer room. Others may volunteer to substitute for a weekly intercessor when needed.

These committed intercessors undergird every aspect of the church in prayer, including the following: each church member, staff, events, mission efforts, and church ministries. Intercessors also pray for the community, national and global concerns, government, and worldwide missions. Biblical prayer guides are an essential resource to keep intercession kingdom focused. Some churches have a telephone line in their prayer room so people can call in prayer requests or ask an intercessor to pray with them. Intercessors may also write prayer grams (notes of prayer) to those who submitted prayer requests.

My (Richard) current church, First Baptist Church of Jonesboro, GA, designated an entire building as a "House of Prayer." The building has various rooms that focus on different aspects of individual or group prayer. Not only does this arrangement facilitate prayer for the church and its concerns, but it provides creative ideas people can implement when they pray at home.

PRAYERWALKING MINISTRY

This ministry provides opportunities for individuals and groups to pray in the specific locations where they want to see God work. We have seen prayer-walking ministries target the areas around a church building or school campus, neighborhoods where they are considering starting a church plant or Bible study, and communities that are experiencing special needs, such as high crime rates, an influx of refugees, or a natural disaster. We are also aware of prayerwalking occurring in many international mission settings. While prayer is not the only ministry churches can carry out in Christ's name, it lays the foundation for subsequent God-honoring ministries.

Prayer Walking in Communist Countries

I (Rick) was part of a prayer-walking team that traveled to a region that had been under communist rule for decades. Our role was to pray in the places we desired to see the Gospel spread. I still remember the spiritual darkness I sensed walking the streets of those neighborhoods. I was tempted to wonder how praying could possibly affect that palpable spiritual darkness. Five years later, I returned to that city. When I stepped out of the airport terminal, a fresh wind of God's presence greeted me. Later, I was moved to tears as I worshipped with a congregation that had formed in the city since our prayer-walking visit. What a blessing to see five adults stand and openly confess Christ at the conclusion of the worship time.

HOMEBOUND INTERCESSORY PRAYER MINISTRY

Participants in this ministry receive payer guides focusing on needs in the church, as well as local, national, and global concerns. These homebound intercessors usually make a commitment to pray at a certain hour of the night or day. This ministry allows people who are not physically able to participate in many church activities to play an important role in God's work. These intercessors should receive updates and reports of answered prayer so they can celebrate God's goodness and maintain fervency in their intercession.

STUDENT PRAYER MINISTRY

This ministry provides numerous opportunities for children and youth to learn about and practice prayer. It can include focused teaching on the biblical principles of prayer, prayer-walking their school campus, and praying for pastoral staff. We have known Student Ministries that set up their own Intercessory Prayer Room with students committing to pray at specific times. For churches to become mighty in prayer, their members must learn to pray at the earliest age possible.

GLOBAL MISSIONS PRAYER MINISTRY

This organized ministry of intercession is specifically focused on local, national, and international missions. Church members commit to pray one hour per week in the Global Missions Prayer Room, which is set up with maps, specific prayer requests from missionaries, urgent prayer requests from national and international mission organizations, and information about unreached people groups. Some Global Prayer Rooms have a computer available for intercessors to engage in virtual prayer walks, read mission newsletters and prayer requests, or send electronic prayer grams to missionaries. This room may be adjacent to the Intercessory Prayer Room, or it can be a distinct area inside the prayer room. If no physical space is available for this ministry, the Prayer Ministry Team can make materials available to intercessors who wish to pray specifically for these concerns.

SPECIAL INTEREST PRAYER GROUPS

These groups of church members gather to pray on a regular basis with a particular focus, such as missions, children, grandchildren, prodigal children, military personnel and their families, physical healing, college students, inmates, or revival. Pastors and Prayer Ministry Coordinators should be sensitive to the specific needs God has laid on the hearts of congregation members. Establishing prayer groups for specific concerns unites church members who share similar burdens to pray together.

Praying for Missions

A church I (Rick) pastored had a Missions Prayer Group that met every Sunday afternoon to pray for missionaries and their work. This prayer group interceded for unreached people groups, our mission partnerships, mission team members' prayer requests, and urgent prayer needs our national and international mission boards sent. Occasionally, a missionary on stateside assignment would speak to the prayer group, then the group would pray over that missionary. This prayer group commissioned any mission team our church sent out, and the mission team would then report what they saw to the prayer group upon returning.

PRAYER GUARDIANS

These intercessors commit to pray for an expectant mother in the church throughout her entire pregnancy and the birth of her baby. These intercessors communicate with the mothers regularly so they are aware of specific needs they might have. We have seen God use this prayer relationship to bring about a long-term relationship between the mother and the intercessor. We have also seen this approach employed for young couples preparing for marriage. An older couple will walk with the engaged couple through their engagement and pre-marital counseling. Often these prayer relationships last for many years after the wedding.

SENIORS INTERCEDING

This prayer ministry involves senior adults who commit to pray for a member of the church's student ministry for one year. This commitment is for prayer, but it can also develop into a friendship or mentorship. A mother once told us how her son had a mowing accident while working at a Christian summer camp. The incident could have been tragic. When her son's senior prayer partner learned of the accident, she told the mother that the day of her son's accident was the day of the week she always prayed for his safety. They rejoiced together for the way God protected this teenager through prayer!

MINISTERS' PRAYER PARTNERS

In this organized ministry of intercession, church members make a year-long commitment to pray for a particular staff member's ministry, personal and spiritual needs, family, and any other prayer requests the minister shares. The prayer partners and ministers meet a minimum of twice annually, perhaps over a meal, for the purpose of fellowship, encouragement, celebrating God's work, and sharing the minister's new prayer needs.

We have also seen church members take time every week to pray over their pastor as he prepares to preach on Sunday. In one church, men gathered around their pastor for an hour on Saturday evening to pray for God's anointing. In many churches, intercessors surround their pastor on Sunday morning to pray before the worship service. What encouragement these prayer times can give a pastor!

Pastoral Prayer Support

As a pastor, I (Rick) experienced so much joy when my prayer partners emailed me or called to ask how they could pray for me that day. I was also diligent about sharing answers to prayer requests I had given them so we could rejoice in God's activity together.

MOMS/GRANDMOTHERS IN PRAYER

For this prayer ministry, a group of women meet on a regular basis to pray for their children and/or grandchildren and their schools. This group can either be an official part of the organization "Moms in Prayer International" (momsinprayer.org) or simply modeled after it. Not only does this ministry provide needed prayer for children, but it offers a wonderful support to mothers who often carry a heavy load.

SPECIAL PRAYER DAYS/EVENTS

Throughout the year, it is important to set aside time to focus on special prayer needs, both locally and nationally. These prayer times give the pastor and congregation an opportunity to seek God's heart together about a common cause.

I (Rick) pastored a church in a community that had seen several teenage deaths in a brief time span. The local sheriff's office called a press conference to announce their plans to keep our teenagers safe. The local school district administration called a press conference to announce their initiative to bring a higher level of security to schools. I realized the one group that had not spoken in the midst of this crisis was the Church. I put out a call for any pastors who desired to join in a communitywide prayer gathering. On a Sunday afternoon, hundreds of believers from multiple denominations gathered at the local high school to cry out to God for our students, families, and community. We experienced a powerful time of worship through scripture, songs, and prayers as the body of Christ showed our community that we believed God had the answer for our teenagers!

CORPORATE PRAYER GATHERINGS

One of the most powerful ways to implement prayer in a local church is through corporate prayer times.

This type of prayer gathering is not the usual mid-week prayer meeting many churches have conducted for decades, but an intentional joining of believers whose agenda is to seek God's heart and mind for a particular issue. In our experience, these gatherings help church members understand the necessity of being a part of a larger family of prayer. While these gatherings may include a brief message from the pastor, the time should be focused on seeking God together as His people.

When I (Richard) first came to a church as its pastor, I discovered that many in the congregation were hurting and confused due to the church's troubled past. We held a prayer gathering on a Friday evening where we sought the Lord for our church's future. We shared what we sensed God was saying as we prayed. That meeting set the tone for the wonderful ministry God granted that church for years afterward.

WORSHIP PRAYER TEAMS

This aspect of prayer ministry may have several distinct expressions. First, the pastor should train members of this team and make them available to anyone desiring prayer during the altar call. In addition, we have seen these teams include rotating small groups who pray during the corporate worship times. You can imagine how encouraged pastors are as they preach knowing a faithful group of people is earnestly praying for the Holy Spirit to work among the congregation. Often, as the pastor extends the altar call, this prayer group will pray specifically and fervently for people to respond to the Holy Spirit's leading.

FINAL THOUGHTS

We have listed these examples, not so you feel overwhelmed or obligated to implement each one in your church, but to demonstrate the rich variety of ways the Prayer Ministry Leadership Team can guide their congregations to become a people devoted to prayer.

Developing a widespread and sustainable prayer culture in a church takes time. A wise pastor and Prayer Ministry Leadership Team will seek the Lord's guidance before initiating new prayer ministries. For the first year, the pastor might meet with the Prayer Ministry Leadership Team regularly to seek God's guidance as to which steps they should take first. Over time, various aspects of the prayer ministry can be gradually added and developed. Obviously, a successful prayer ministry must be built, sustained, and empowered by prayer!

We can testify that in our broad ministry experience and travels, we have never seen a church with a vibrant prayer ministry that was not also seeing God work powerfully in its midst. Prayer is worth the effort, because prayer brings the power of almighty God to bear on an individual and a congregation. Never underestimate what God can do through a praying church!

CONCLUSION

We hope that in this brief overview, God has inspired you to do whatever is necessary to develop your congregation into a powerful, praying church. It will undoubtedly involve a process. It is unlikely to occur as the result of one sermon on prayer or an announcement of a new prayer initiative. Praying churches are most likely to be found where there are praying pastors. So begin with yourself. Earnestly seek to deepen your intercession until God is pleased to mobilize heaven as a result of your prayers. We can assure you that when your people witness mountains moving as a result of your intercession, there will soon be others who seek to join you in prayer.

The key is not to grow discouraged before your people become earth-shaking intercessors. In 1857, Jeremiah Lanphier earnestly desired to lead businesspeople in New York City to pray. Initially, few showed interest in the endeavor. But then the floodgates burst. More than 50,000 people were soon praying during the noon hour across the city. Revival swept out of those meetings and spread across the land. In one year, more than one million people in America were converted. One person felt led to make prayer a priority, and as a result, America experienced one of the greatest spiritual awakenings in its history.

Developing your congregation into a praying people requires patience, determination, and a robust prayer life of your own. But it is well worth every effort. For once your people have learned to cry out to God, absolutely anything is possible.

QUESTIONS FOR CONSIDERATION

1. How would you evaluate your current praying in public? Is it inspiring others to want to pray? How could it be improved?

2. What are some specific ways you could teach prayer to your people from the pulpit? Is there a particular series that would be helpful?

3. Have you been diligent in helping others to pray in a God-honoring manner during worship services? If not, what are some practical steps you could take to help people pray more effectively in public?

4. Is there a Prayer Ministry Leadership Team or Prayer Ministry Coordinator in your church?

5. What specific prayer ministries is God impressing upon you to begin in your church?

APPENDIX 1

Prayer Ministry Organization in the Local Church

PASTOR

PRAYER MINISTRY COORDINATOR

PRAYER MINISTRY LEADERSHIP TEAM

Teach and Equip

Annual Prayer Conferences   Discipleship Courses on Prayer
Resources and Prayer Guides
Sermon Series on Prayer

Mobilize

Prayerwalking Ministry   Special Interest Prayer Groups
Moms/Grandmothers in Prayer   Special Prayer Days/Events
Seniors Interceding   Ministers' Prayer Partners
Student Prayer Ministry   Prayer Guardians
Corporate Prayer Gatherings   Global Missions Prayer Ministry
Worship Prayer Teams   Homebound Prayer Ministry
Intercessory Ministry/Prayer Room

Teach and Equip: Teach the Biblical principles of prayer, making tools and resources available along with opportunities to grow in the knowledge/experience of personal and corporate prayer

Mobilize: Provide specific opportunities for people to put into practice what they are learning and "plug into" the prayer life of the church according to their interests and passions

BIBLIOGRAPHY

As the pastor leads the congregation to become a house of prayer, there is a plethora of resources available. We have listed here those books that have impacted our lives and the churches we have served over the past 40 years.

DEVOTIONAL BOOKS

Arthur, Kay. *His Imprint, My Expression*

Bennett, Arthur. *The Valley of Vision: A Collection of Puritan Prayers*

Blackaby, Henry and Richard. *Being Still*

Blackaby, Henry and Richard. *Experiencing God Day by Day*

Chambers, Oswald. *My Utmost for His Highest*

Fuller, Cheri and Dean, Jennifer Kennedy. *The One Year of Praying the Promises of God*

Hughes, Selwyn. *Every Day with Jesus*

Hughes, Selwyn. *Prayer, the Greatest Power*

Lucado, Max. *God's Inspirational Promise Book*

Murray, Andrew. *Teach Me to Pray*

Myers, Ruth. *31 Days of Praise*

Myers, Ruth. *31 Days of Power*

Shepherd, J. Barrie. *Diary of Daily Prayer*

Spurgeon, Charles. *Faith's Check Book*

Thornton, Henry. *Devotional Prayers*

BOOKS ON PRAYER

Batterson, Mark. *The Circle Maker*

Berndt, Jodie. *Praying the Scriptures for Your Children*

Blackaby, Henry and Norman. *Experiencing Prayer with Jesus*

Blackaby, Henry and Richard. *Hearing God's Voice*

Boa, Kenneth. *Face to Face: Praying the Scriptures for Intimate Worship*

Boa, Kenneth. *Face to Face: Praying the Scriptures for Spiritual Growth*

Bounds, E.M. *Power Through Prayer*

Bounds, E.M. *Prayer and Praying Men*

Bounds, E.M. *The Necessity of Prayer*

Crawford, Dan R. *The Prayer-Shaped Disciple*

Cymbala, Jim. *Fresh Wind, Fresh Fire*

Dean, Jennifer Kennedy. *The Praying Life*

Dean, Jennifer Kennedy. *Legacy of Prayer*

Dean, Jennifer Kennedy. *Heart's Cry*

Dean, Jennifer Kennedy. *Power Praying*

Duewel, Wesley. *Ablaze for God*

Duewel, Wesley. *Mighty Prevailing Prayer*

Foster, Richard J. *Celebration of Discipline*

Franklin, John. *And the Place was Shaken: How to Lead a Powerful Prayer Meeting*

Frizzell, Greg. *Returning to Holiness*

Gordon, S.D. *Quiet Talks on Prayer*

Hallesby, O. *Prayer*

Helms, Elaine. *Prayer without Limits*

Henderson, Daniel. *Old Paths New Power*

Henderson, Daniel. *Transforming Prayer*

Hybels, Bill. *Too Busy Not to Pray*

Kendrick, Alex and Stephen. *Battle Plan for Prayer*

Kopp, David. *Praying the Bible for Your Life*

Lessin, Roy. *Promises to Pray Over Your Children*

Lotz, Anne Graham. *The Daniel Prayer*

Moody, Dwight. *Prevailing Prayer*

Moore, Beth. *Praying God's Word*

Murray, Andrew. *Power in Prayer*

Murray, Andrew. *Prayer's Inner Chamber*

Murray, Andrew. *With Christ in the School of Prayer*

Omartian, Stormie. *The Power of a Praying Wife*

Omartian, Stormie. *The Power of a Praying Parent*

Omartian, Stormie. *The Prayer that Changes Everything*

Sacks, Cheryl. *The Prayer Saturated Church*

Sheets, Dutch. *How to Pray for Lost Loved Ones*

Shirer, Priscilla. *Fervent*

Spurgeon, Charles. *The Power in Prayer*

Stewart, George S. *The Lower Levels of Prayer*

Whitney, Donald S. *Spiritual Disciplines for the Christian Life*

Wood, Tony. *A Parent's Book of Prayers*

ABOUT THE AUTHORS

 **Dr. Richard Blackaby** has been a pastor, a seminary president, and is currently the president of Blackaby Ministries International. He has coauthored numerous books with his father, Henry, including: *Experiencing God: Revised Edition, Spiritual Leadership: Moving People on to God's Agenda, Fresh Encounter, Hearing God's Voice, Experiencing God: Day by Day, Called to Be God's Leader: Lessons from the Life of Joshua, Being Still With God, God in the Marketplace* and *Flickering Lamps: Christ and His Church.* He also authored: *Putting a Face on Grace: Living a Life Worth Passing On, Unlimiting God, The Seasons of God, Experiencing God at Home, The Inspired Leader, and Rebellious Parenting: Daring to Break the Rules So Your Child Can Thrive* and *Living Out of the Overflow: Serving Out of Your Intimacy with God.* Richard works with Christian CEOs of corporate America and speaks internationally on various topics including spiritual leadership in the church, the home, and the marketplace.

You can follow him at:

Twitter: @richardblackaby
Facebook: Dr Richard Blackaby.

 **Rev. Rick Fisher** serves as Vice President for Blackaby Ministries International. He and his wife Debbie, live in Easley, South Carolina and have two daughters, Jamie and Betsy, sons-in-law Rob and Lucas, and five grandchildren – Thomas, Ashley, Jase and Leighton and Gray.

Rick earned a BA in Religion from Gardner Webb University and a Masters degree in Religious Education from Southern Baptist Theological Seminary. He has served 30+ years of ministry in the local church (18 years of that as Senior Pastor) and has been part of the BMI team since 2010. During his years as a senior pastor, Rick led each church to be a strong house of prayer with a variety of prayer expressions that served as a spiritual foundation for the ministry of the congregation.

Rick speaks to churches, associations and in marketplace settings with focuses in the areas of spiritual leadership, revival/awakening and prayer.

You can follow him at:

Twitter: @rickfisher54
Facebook: Rick Fisher

Blackaby Revitalization Ministry

If you sense God wants more for your church than what you are currently experiencing, we want to help. It may well be that you have been doing everything you know to do. But that's not enough. You need to do what GOD knows you should do! You must seek Him for those answers. We can help pastors as well as church members seek a fresh word and direction from God. Let us help you experience a fresh encounter with the risen Christ so you are prepared for the great work God wants to do through your church.

Two resources that can help are the book *Flickering Lamps: Christ and His Church* and the *Flickering Lamps DVD* set. Working in conjunction with one another, these resources will help you discover God's truths for struggling, discouraged churches.

To learn more, go to **http://www.blackaby.net/revitalization/home/** or email us at **information@blackaby.org**

Blackaby Leadership Coaching

Blackaby Ministries provides coaching-based solutions to challenges faced by ministry and marketplace leaders. We also help teams achieve the focus and harmony that God intends. To learn more, go to **www.blackabycoaching.org** or email us at **information@blackaby.org**

For more information about peer coaching cohorts for pastors and ministry leaders along with information about our three day coach training workshops, visit **www.blackabycoaching.org**

Living Out of the Overflow

This book is written for the many Christians who have experienced "dry" periods in their life. Many Christian souls have become barren and parched due to life's trials and burdens.

The irony is that Christians have living water available within them! In the pages of "Overflow", Dr. Richard Blackaby shares a treasure trove of biblical truths that can help you experience living water each day as you abide in Christ and as you serve Him.

We invite you to walk alongside Moses and Elijah and see how they ultimately learned to live and lead out of the overflow of their personal walk with God.

As you read these pages, may you find refreshing and nourishment and be empowered to undertake God's assignment for you. God doesn't just want you to survive. He wants you to live and minister out of the overflow of His abundance.

To learn more, email us at **information@blackaby.org**

Recommendation:

Whether serving as a senior pastor, seminary president or president of Blackaby Ministries International, Richard Blackaby is a visible demonstration of what it means to be *Living Out of the Overflow*. His new book of the same title is one that should bless those who may be living minimally, yet long to live in God's abundance.

— ANNE GRAHAM LOTZ, President and Founder of AnGeL Ministries

Apply the truths of *Experiencing God* to every area of your church

Experiencing God: Knowing and Doing the Will of God

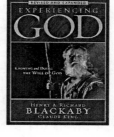

Henry Blackaby, Richard Blackaby and Claude King guide believers through seven Scriptural realities that teach us how to develop a true relationship with the Creator. By understanding how God is working through us even as we try to fathom His ways, we can begin to clearly know and do His will and discover our lives greatly and gracefully changed.

Member Book
Leader's Kit (DVDs)

Your Church Experiencing God Together

Henry and Mel Blackaby demonstrate God's plan for all believers to utilize their spiritual gifts as part of a loving church body, under Christ's headship, empowered by the Holy Spirit to become a world mission strategy center.

Member Book
DVDs

When God Speaks

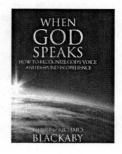

Henry and Richard Blackaby help believers to understand God does speak to His followers and that He gives clear, personal instructions that enable believers to experience fully His power, presence, and love.

Member Book

Experiencing God as Couples

Henry and Marilynn Blackaby lead married couples to experience God's presence in a way that will last a lifetime. This study has influenced thousands of lives, resulting in saved marriages, spouses coming to Jesus, rededications, couples volunteering for missions, and enriched marriages.
Member Book
DVDs

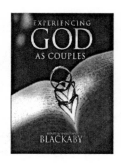

The Man God Uses: Moved from the Ordinary to the Extraordinary

Henry and Tom Blackaby provide men with a study that is designed to provide spiritual direction and encouragement. Men are being touched by God all over, and men who have encountered God need to understand what He is doing in their lives and what their lives can mean when turned over to God.
Member Book
DVDs

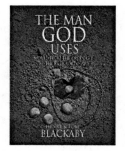

The Family God Uses: Becoming a Home of Influence

Tom and Kim Blackaby show parents how to discover where God is at work around their family and to learn how to join Him in that work. Use this resource to get and keep your family God-centered and teach your children their role in His kingdom.
Member Book

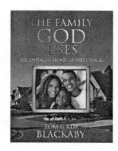

Contact us for special discounted pricing on Blackaby resources!
PO Box 1035; Jonesboro, GA 30237-1035;
phone toll free 1-877-311-2626;
email *resources@blackaby.org*; or order online at *www.blackaby.org*

Blackaby Ministries International (www.blackaby.org)
is dedicated to helping people experience God. It has
books and resources to assist Christians in the areas
of experiencing God, spiritual leadership, revival, the
marketplace, and the family. There are also resources for
young adults and children. Please contact them at:

Facebook:	Blackaby Ministries International
Twitter:	@ExperiencingGod
Mobile App:	Blackaby ministries int
Website:	www.blackaby.org